Sherlock Holmes and Dr. Crippen

The North London Cellar Murder (the 'crime of the century') as recorded by Dr. John H. Watson

by
Donald MacLachlan

First published in 2019 by
The Irregular Special Press
for Baker Street Studios Ltd
Endeavour House
170 Woodland Road, Sawston
Cambridge, CB22 3DX, UK

ISBN: 1-901091-72-4 (10 digit)
ISBN: 978-1-901091-72-4 (13 digit)

Front Cover Illustration: Public domain image of Harvey Hawley Crippen
originally published in 1910. Copyright expired.

Back Cover Illustration: Public domain image of Harvey Hawley Crippen and Ethel
Clara Neave on trial in the Old Bailey, Number One Court, 1910.

Typeset in 8/11/20pt Palatino

To my late mother, and my late step-dad. Gabrielle Ruth Hermitte first married my father, Alastair Robert Anderson MacLachlan. A bomber pilot, he was shot down and killed over Germany in 1943. Later, long after the war, she married my stepfather, Philip King, surgeon. Sadly, both are long gone. My thanks to them for so much …

About the Author

Sheffield-born Donald MacLachlan's interests in Sherlock Holmes and Dr. John H. Watson came after a ride on a London Underground train in 1955, when he was 13 and his family lived in Earl's Court.

The eastbound District Line train from Earl's Court went through what was then an open triangle of land bounded by the Earl's Court, Gloucester Road and High Street Kensington stations. (Later, the triangle was covered from 1957-84 by the BEA West London Air Terminal, and the site now houses a Sainsburys shop.)

This triangle, Donald thought, must be where foreign spy Hugo Oberstein supposedly heaved the body of Arthur Cadogan West onto the roof of a briefly stationary Circle Line train. This in the Sherlockian tale *The Adventure of the Bruce-Partington Plans*.

Donald found that 'Caulfield Gardens', Oberstein's street, did not exist under that name. But there were indeed houses with rear windows that overlooked the Underground tracks (although the story confuses the issue of exactly *which* track.) Happily ignoring all the *No Trespassing* and *Danger* signs, and carefully crossing the live rails, Donald explored the area. Only to determine that it would take a man of superhuman strength to toss a body onto the roof of a train anywhere there.

That led to further and deeper interest into the Holmesian stories. Then, later, he heard how Jeremy Potter, chairman of the Richard III Society from 1971-89, had invited a senior member of the Sherlock Holmes Society of London to a Richard III Society dinner. That, in turn, led Donald to a study of Richard III, and the thought that Richard's *alleged* murder of The Two Little Princes in the Tower was a mystery worthy of Mr. Holmes (or, indeed, of Dr. Watson.)

A move to Canada in 1962, and a journalism career that ended in 1993, interfered with further research. During a subsequent career in public relations (the last stop as director of public affairs and media relations for Canada's Simon Fraser University) he gathered boxes of books and research material, and in 2007 began bit by bit to write this book. It was published in 2013 by Baker Street Studios Ltd., under the title of *The Adventure of the Bloody Tower*. (ISBN: 978 1901091 59 5)

Now retired, Donald and wife Cailleach (who is herself working on a historical novel about the Glencoe Massacre of 1692) live in White Rock, British Columbia, with 19 large bookcases – and more of them in mind. He is a member of the Sherlock Holmes Society of London and of several Richard III societies.

Chapter One

-------- --

Mr. Sherlock Holmes was officially retired, and, supposedly, ardently studying bees on the southern slope of the Downs. I use the word 'retired' with a warm smile, however, as my friend was, as he put it to me, "occasionally somewhat *un*-retired", which meant (I was certain) that he was as active in the secret service of our new king as he had been for the old, and for the queen before that.

Mr. Holmes had continued to maintain, as a London *pied à terre*, our old, well worn, and comfortable lodgings at 221B, Baker Street. He sometimes stayed there for weeks at a time, with a Sussex neighbour caring for his bees, and making notes, in Mr. Holmes's daily log, on their varied behaviours. I came up from Southsea much less frequently myself, but we were there together, as of old, on the chilly evening of Wednesday the 29th of June, 1910, when we had a caller.

The man was a stranger to me, but clearly not one to Mr. Holmes. To my surprise, they greeted each other as if they were two music-hall comedians performing a well-worn but still popular routine on the stage.

"How do you *dew*," inquired Mr. Holmes, with exaggerated emphasis on the last word.

"I *dew* very well," replied the stranger. "Are you at *Holmes* to visitors?"

Both men laughed immoderately.

Our visitor was clean-cut, handsome, alert, of average height (perhaps 5' 9") but of strong build, and in his forties. His face was a little angular. His brown hair was greying, and receding above a high forehead. His generous moustache was neatly combed and waxed. His suit was brown, a little tweedy for the city, perhaps; well fitting enough but not expensive. He had an air of authority and confidence. Years ago, I might well have declared him to be a military man. Now, after considerable experience and training under Mr. Sherlock Holmes, and watching the way our visitor's eyes steadily roamed the room and took in details, and from the way he selected and positioned a chair so that he could face the door, I was able quickly to conclude that he was a policeman. And, I thought, all in all, very probably an inspector, perhaps a chief inspector.

Mr. Holmes turned to me. "Watson, you have not met my old friend Chief Inspector Walter Dew of New Scotland Yard. He has quite often visited us here, but somehow you have always managed to be absent. Let us make up for that now. Dew, may I introduce my longtime colleague and most valued partner, Dr. John Watson?"

Dew seized my hand with a firm grip.

"I have heard of you often," said he, with a warm smile. "I understand that Mr. Holmes would be as lost without you as I would be without Arthur Mitchell, my sergeant."

"Thank you," I returned. "I have often heard of you, too, from Mr. Holmes. Walter Dew, the man who arrested Harry the Valet. I am proud and delighted to meet you at last."

Dew laughed, and continued. "Harry the Valet, yes. Please hold onto that memory of me. All that engages me these days is a daily mountain of forms and paperwork, and a routine case involving an actress of apparently modest talent whose friends are concerned about her sudden disappearance. Off to America whence she came, it seems. A married woman; a case of *cherchez l'homme*, I expect."

Mr. Holmes brought him a glass, and handed me a neat whisky as well. The chief inspector sipped his drink thoughtfully.

"Well, Holmes, after hearing that you were still here in town, I dropped by to tell you that I have definitely decided to retire. Police work is not what it used to be, as you well know. Too much paper. Too many reports. Far too much internal bickering and posturing at New Scotland Yard, and far too few interesting cases. And there is that private reason of which you already know, Holmes. It will be a bit of a difficult go financially, I fear, but Kate and I are determined, and we shall manage. I think that I may very well join your profession as a private inquiry consultant."

Mr. Holmes nodded sympathetically. "You do not surprise me, on any of those counts. Will you dine with us?"

"If I may, thank you, although I hope you do not think that I turned up at this hour in the hope of being invited. Kate is away in the country visiting relatives, though, and my children used to say that, when it comes to cooking, I am a most excellent blacksmith. So Mrs. Hudson's cooking would be much appreciated.

"You are invited only if our good landlady's larder will stretch to three. I shall go and ask her."

As Mr. Holmes's footsteps thumped hurriedly down the stairs, I turned to Dew to begin the conversation that, as the acting host, good manners required of me.

"Harry the Valet," I began. "You were the man who caught Harry the Valet, the French jewel thief."

"I thank you again for remembering," Dew returned. "I did work on the case. An English jewel thief, though, in truth. Bill Johnson, his name was. Or Williams. Or Villiers, or James, or Wilson. Quite a character."

"The Duchess of Sutherland's jewels; correct?"

"Indeed. Worth a fortune, too: twenty-five or thirty thousand pounds. Taken from her luggage on a train in Paris. Shopped by an angry woman, Harry was, and then we got him, back here in London, in South Kensington. We got some of the jewels back, but only a few, though. The rest were gone."

Mr. Holmes re-entered the room, and confirmed the invitation for dinner. "You are telling Watson of the

Sutherland jewel theft? A successful little raid you made in Cathcart Road, I recall. Tell the good doctor the story."

Dew settled back proudly into his chosen basket chair, and began.

"I was a new inspector at the time, October '98. The Duchess of Sutherland was *en route* to London from the Riviera. She discovered as her train left Paris that her jewel case had vanished. More than 40 pieces of jewellery had gone. Worth a fortune, as I say.

"Inspector Walter Dinnie and I – the Walters Brothers, they called us – began to investigate some of our best-known British thieves, and especially our British jewel thieves: Where were they at the time of the theft? Had they been abroad? Could they have been abroad? Meanwhile, the French police were doing the same with their list of known jewel thieves.

"We soon learnt that Harry the Valet, a smooth and crafty London thief well known to Inspector Dinnie, had come in to money. He was flush, and throwing lots of cash about, here in London, and buying champagne. We went looking for him, but he simply disappeared. We concluded that he had become aware of our interest him and had bolted. We actually had no evidence that linked him with the theft, but we spread the word in the underworld that we much wanted to find Harry, and that we would look kindly upon the man who led us to him.

"In the end, though, it was a woman who gave us the first useful evidence. She was an actress, and a former lover of Harry. She had been in Paris that October, and said that Harry had brought a fine cache of jewels to her flat there, and allowed her to wear some of them. She suspected that they were stolen, of course, and Harry confirmed it.

"The pair had a nasty falling out, though, and, in her rage and fury, she told the French police about the jewels, and told them all about Harry.

"If the Frenchies tried to find him, they were unsuccessful, and Harry made it back to London.

"It was some time before we at New Scotland Yard got a solid tip, and that led us to a flat at 5, Cathcart Road. We armed ourselves with a revolver, as we knew that Harry could be a violent man. "Would you believe that the key had been left in the front door of the building? So that was no problem, and in we crept, three of us, and up to Harry's floor. But now we would have to smash our way into Harry's flat. Carefully, and quietly, I turned the handle – to find that this door was also unlocked, and not bolted! Another stroke of good luck. And in we barged.

"Harry gave up without a struggle, and we recovered some of the stolen jewels there. He even had three fine diamonds in his waistcoat pocket, and three hundred and twenty pounds in cash on him. Harry pleaded guilty, and got sentenced to seven years. We never did recover any more of the jewels, though."

Mr. Holmes shook his head. "You say you are working on the case of an actress who has vanished? The same actress?"

"Not the same, no," returned Dew. "And I am not actually working on the case; not yet. The missing woman's friends are old acquaintances of Frosty, and have an appointment with him tomorrow. You know that he can never say no. I expect that he will ask me to take it on."

Mr. Holmes chuckled, and addressed me. "Frosty, Watson, is Superintendent Frank Froest, Dew's senior officer. He was, by the way, one of the three officers who arrested Harry the Valet in South Kensington. Have you a sixpence in your pocket?"

Now Dew chuckled.

"Sixpence?" I inquired. "A sixpenny coin?

I delved obediently into a trousers pocket. "Here you are, Holmes, my very last sixpence."

"Hang onto it, my dear fellow. Now, hold it between your right thumb, and your index finger, as if you were going to try to bend it between them" I so held it.

"Now, Watson, *do* bend it," commanded Mr. Holmes. "Squeeze it with all your brute strength until it bends. Indeed, break it if you can."

I duly strained and squeezed, suffering some considerable pain and discomfort, but the sixpence remained stubbornly unbent and unbroken.

"It is not possible," I reported. Both men laughed again.

Dew shook his head. "It is possible for Superintendent Froest, Doctor. He has the strongest hands of any man alive, I am sure. He can snap a sixpence like a halfpenny biscuit. Why, he can tear a pack of playing cards in two with his bare hands. I have seen him do it, often.

"The question now, I suppose, is what is in the cards for me. Looking for a missing actress, who may not be missing at all, sounds like a tiresome bore. No wonder I am ready for my pension."

Little did we suspect then that Dew's 'tiresome bore' would, in fact, turn out to be one of England's most fascinating, horrific and gruesome criminal cases, and one most avidly followed by newspapers and their shocked and intrigued readers around the world.

Chapter Two

Chief Inspector Dew visited us again briefly on July 1st, the day after his meeting with Superintendent Froest and the friends of the missing actress.

"Well, I am indeed on the case of the missing woman. Frosty's friends, who brought the case to us, are John Edward Nash and his wife Lillian. He is a theatrical manager. She is a music-hall performer who uses the stage-name of Lil Hawthorne; the Hawthorne Sisters act. The Nashes have been investigating the reported death in America of their missing friend, who is another music-hall performer, if not a very successful one."

"Music hall?" I inquired. "I know, or know of, a few people in the trade. Who is the missing woman?

"She uses the stage-name of Belle Elmore. Her real name is Cora Crippen, an American, and the wife of an American doctor here in London, Hawley Harvey Crippen; or perhaps he is a dentist; I am not clear as to which."

"Crippen? Not a name to me. Nor Belle Elmore. The Hawthorne Sisters I know of, but have never actually seen." I reached to the old bookshelf for our medical directory. "No Dr. Crippen is shown in here."

Dew picked up his story again: "This Crippen told them that his wife had left hastily for America on February 1st, and that she had died of pneumonia there, in the city of Los Angeles, on March 23rd. Mr. and Mrs. Nash are most

13

concerned, and have grave doubts about Crippen's story. They are sure that they have caught him in several lies, and they begin to that fear his wife may even have met with foul play.

"First, they and their other variety friends say that it is absolutely inconceivable that this Belle Elmore would have left for America, under any circumstance, without letting them know. And equally inconceivable that in her weeks there she would not have written to her many friends. She was a friendly and vivacious person and meticulous about keeping in touch, and sending letters and postcards. She would never have left London without visiting her friends to say goodbye, or inviting them to her house for a farewell party. She would never have taken passage on a ship without sending postcards to everyone. Nor would she have travelled across America without writing at length to her friends. They are unanimous and adamant upon these points.

"Some others of her friends made inquiries, seeking to determine when she left England and on what ship. They could not find Mrs. Crippen on any list of passengers, under that name or as Belle Elmore. Nor could they confirm what ship she might have sailed on. Crippen apparently gave them a name of a French ship, but they may have misheard it, or mangled it. The one they thought he *might have* named turned out to have been out of service.

"Dr. Crippen said that she became ill *en route* to California, and died in Los Angeles, at the home of his son by an earlier marriage, Otto Crippen. But the friends' inquiries to that city found no such death on record there. They did eventually get in touch with Crippen's son, and *he* said that, according to his father, Belle Elmore had actually died in San Francisco. They have since pursued that, with no luck at all.

"Then we have on March 26th a notice in *The Era*, a theatrical newspaper, recording Mrs. Crippen's death in California: 'Elmore – 23 March, in California USA, Miss Belle Elmore (Mrs. H. H. Crippen.)' They are quite sure that Crippen placed it. I agree – who else could it be? – and we are confirming that."

14

Dew hesitated. "I have kept my account to the minimum for an embarrassing reason. The Nashes know of your skills, and wonder if they may consult you in your professional capacity. Nash would like to tell you his story in person. Would you accept?"

Mr. Holmes nodded. "Not at all my kind of case, but if it would help you, I should be happy to."

Dew smiled with relief. "Well, it is always possible that you may turn up something that I have missed and, after all, it is really on behalf of Frosty. You have dealt with him before, and there is no harm in keeping him happy. I am glad, then, that I have given you only a barebones version of Nash's story, so as to leave you with a clean slate.

Dew paused again. "To conclude my tale for today, here comes the finishing touch: They say that Crippen has been keeping close company with his typist, one Ethel Clara Le Neve. According to them, Crippen is aged forty-seven, and this Miss Le Neve is a good twenty years younger.

"They add that on February 20th, only nineteen days after Mrs. Crippen supposedly left for America, this Le Neve woman accompanied Crippen to a ball of the Music Hall Ladies' Benevolent Fund – and that she was wearing furs and jewels that people there were sure they recognised as Mrs. Crippen's furs and jewels that she apparently left behind upon her departure for America.

"So wherever his wife has gone, Dr. Crippen seems to be enjoying her absence. A bit dangerously, as well; taking Le Neve to a ball that all of his wife's music-hall friends attended.

"The Nashes say that Mrs. Crippen had a special friend of some kind, an American music-hall man here in London. He returned to the United States some time ago. They propose this as a theory: Crippen has this younger mistress. Belle Elmore found out about it, and has run off with her own lover. The Nashes do not believe that she would have run away like that, but their guess would be that she *has* run off, and that Crippen is trying in some extraordinary and hurtful way to salvage some respect, and save face, by claiming first that his wife was ill, and then that she had died."

Mr. Holmes now took us both by surprise.

"She may very well *be* dead," he declared.

"Not sure I follow," said a frowning Dew.

Mr. Holmes shook his head, gently and patiently, and explained.

"Her friends say that she meticulously sends letters and postcards. Now Dr. Crippen tells them that she is dead. He must know, then, that there is absolutely no chance that she will be sending to her acquaintances any more letters and postcards to contradict him. He must know, too, that she is not going to turn up on one of their doorsteps.

"*Ergo*, she is indeed dead, or, at least, has inexplicably cut off all her friends – and Crippen knows that she is no longer going to resume her relations with them."

"Oh, right," responded Dew, slowly. "I see. Of course. So perhaps she really did die in America."

"That we do not know," returned Mr. Holmes. "But if she is still alive, why has she suddenly stopped corresponding with her friends?"

Dew pursed his lips. "If she has gone away to this American lover, that might preclude her from writing, or at least discourage her."

"Permanently? In perpetuity? Crippen is extraordinarily sure that she is not going to write to anybody again, or ever again turn up to visit them."

Dew rose hastily from his chair.

"I think, Holmes, that you are telling me that Detective Sergeant Mitchell and I had better get to work, and at full speed."

Chapter Three

John Nash called upon us by appointment at Baker Street the following day, Saturday July 2nd, and engaged us in a confident and forceful style that I have found common in Americans (as the Nashes are).

Nash assailed me instantly. "Chief Inspector Dew tells me, Dr. Watson, that you are a disciple of the English music hall. I should be very happy to arrange for tickets for you to any show that you desire. I have many connections in the business."

I smiled. "Disciple is too strong a word, but I certainly went to the Shoreditch Music Hall a few times when I was a medical student. Since then, I have been known on occasion to visit Sam Collins's establishment, and the two Palaces, Hammersmith and Shaftesbury Avenue. I have not been to Hammersmith, though, since its alterations and re-opening earlier this year."

Mr. Nash frowned. "They are showing the moving pictures there now, of course, and at the Shaftesbury. There are fewer of the old acts on the boards. I fear that it will not be long before this invention of moving pictures much changes our way of life as entertainers."

I shared a frown with him. "I regret that I have never been able to attend one of your wife's performances."

"Oh, you have missed much. I am her manager, of course, so we must take the first opportunity for you to hear her song *Tell me if you love me.*"

Nash now looked directly at Mr. Holmes, and, finally taking a seat, began his tale.

"I am no detective, Mr. Holmes, but a man of observation and action nonetheless. Let me begin at the beginning. My wife and I have known Belle Elmore, Mrs. Crippen, for quite a few years.

"As it happens, we attended a private New Year's Eve celebration at their home last December 31st, along with Melinda May, who is the secretary of the Music Hall Ladies' Guild. She and Belle were members of the committee of that organization. Belle was a real artiste at raising funds for the Guild, to be used in support of unfortunate women and children in the music-hall world.

"The evening was pleasurable. The Crippens are very good hosts, she in the leading rôle of hostess and he as a quiet, supporting host, anxious to please all. Those rôles suited their characters well. Belle was always a lively and enthusiastic chatterbox; anyone she met she instantly treated as a lifelong friend. The doctor was more reserved and mild, a milquetoast, some would say; not really a man's man, perhaps, but always pleasant and obliging.

"Move on now to February of this year. On February 2nd, Belle missed a meeting of the Music Hall Ladies' Guild, and did so without notice. This was not at all like her. Then my wife heard that Belle had resigned as honorary treasurer of the Guild. We knew no more than that, and did not know why. We did not then know that the reason was Belle's departure for the States; we thought she was in London, of course. So we sent a telegram to Belle's home and proposed that we get together on the Saturday, the fifth of February. My Lil was desperate to ask Belle to change her mind and to carry on as treasurer. However, we got no reply.

"The Guild sent her a letter offering to keep the post of treasurer open for her, but got no reply to that, either. Now this did strike us as unusual, if not in fact downright strange, as Belle would normally never fail to answer a letter or a telegram; not a chance.

"Now we have all been told by Dr. Crippen that Belle had not only resigned but had actually left for the States on February 2nd, the day of the Guild meeting, because a relative there was ill. We knew that she had family there, sure. It seemed, though, that the two letters of resignation the Guild then received were not written by her, but by Dr. Crippen. Looking back, I should have realised that was odd, that she would not write her own letters to her own friends of the Guild, on such a significant matter.

"Here is a copy of the first of those two letters, which was sent on February 2nd to Melinda May, the Guild secretary. It was delivered to her by the Le Neve woman, Crippen's so-called typist. I'll come back to her in a minute. Melinda is firm that it was not in Belle Elmore's hand-writing, and, as you can see, it bore Crippen's initials as the writer."

Nash handed to Mr. Holmes a document that my friend read aloud.

39, Hilldrop Crescent,

February 2nd.

Dear Miss May,

Illness of a near relative has called me to America on only a few hours' notice, so I must ask you to bring my resignation as treasurer before the meeting to-day, so that a new treasurer can be elected at once. You will appreciate my haste when I tell you that I have not been to bed all night packing, and getting ready to go. I shall hope to see you again a few months later, but cannot spare a moment to call on you before I go. I wish you everything nice till I return to London again.

Now, good-bye, with love hastily,

Yours,

Belle Elmore, p.p. H. H. C.

19

Nash gave Mr. Holmes a second sheet of paper. "Then we have this second letter, delivered at the same time by Miss Le Neve, purporting to confirm the resignation and including the Guild's bank deposit book and cheque book. It was in the same hand-writing as the first – not Belle's – but this time did not have Crippen's initials on it."

Again, Mr. Holmes read it aloud, as he often did when committing documents to memory.

39, Hilldrop Crescent,
London, N.

To the Committee of the Music Hall Ladies' Guild.

Dear Friends,

Please forgive me a hasty letter and any inconvenience I may cause you, but I have just had news of the illness of a near relative and at only a few hours' notice I am obliged to go to America. Under the circumstances I cannot return for several months, and therefore beg you to accept this as a formal letter resigning from this date my hon. treasurership of the M.H.L.G.

I am enclosing the cheque book and deposit book for the immediate use of my successor, and to save any delay I beg to suggest that you vote to suspend the usual rules of election and elect to-day a new honorary treasurer.

I hope some months later to be with you again, and in meantime wish the Guild every success and ask my good friends and pals to accept my sincere and loving wishes for their own personal welfare.

Believe me, yours faithfully,

Belle Elmore

Nash held up a cautionary hand. "We were not suspicious at this point. That came later."

Mr. Holmes and I nodded, and I refilled Nash's glass. The music-hall man leaned forward in his chair as he continued his account.

"Some of Belle's other friends caught up to Crippen, and asked what had happened to Belle. He said she had gone to the States on a legal matter. We all took that to mean that Belle's relative had died, and that Belle had headed there in connection with the estate. But why had she not said goodbye to her friends? Why had she not written to them and to the Guild? Crippen said that she had been too busy packing and making her arrangements to leave.

"On February 7th, Crippen visited Clara and Paul Martinetti, two other members of the Guild, and Clara just let him have it: Even if Belle had not been able to tell her friends, why had Crippen himself not let people know? Crippen replied that nobody had had any time; he was sorting out some legal papers while Belle was doing the packing.

"Again, we were not suspicious yet. We took his story in good faith, even when he told the Martinettis and Melinda May that Belle had become ill on her way to California.

"But we did wonder: If she had been in touch with Crippen from the States, to let him know that she was sick, why had she not been in touch with any of her friends? That we did not understand. Crippen himself said that he did not know why, and that he did not understand it himself.

"We said that we hoped that Belle would visit our friend Isabel Ginnett in New York. Isabel is a former president of the Guild. We knew that she was staying in New York while her husband was on tour."

I interrupted. "Would that be Fred Ginnett? The horseman? The 'Dick Turpin's Ride to York' act?"

Nash laughed. "Yes, sure. That's the man. You are more of a disciple than you admit."

Nash now frowned and spoke heavily. "Crippen said that, no, Belle would not be visiting New York. She was going straight to California to deal with some legal business about the relative.

"I would say that, at this point in time, we were still very much puzzled. Why had Belle not written to any of us? Why would she not stop in New York to see Isabel? And Belle had family in New York; surely she would stop off to see them en route to California. It was all very odd, and very unlike Belle. But I suppose we could understand that, if she had been called away urgently, she might have not had time to let us all know she was going.

"All right, you understand, but the suspicions of something being very much amiss began for us in spades on February 20th, when my wife and I, and many of our friends, attended the Guild Ball at the Criterion.

"There was Crippen, accompanied by a rather plain young woman, much younger than him, who was introduced to me and the others as his typist. That was the Le Neve woman, of course. I tell you: The way they looked at each other was not the way the boss looks at his typist, and *vice versa*. I know what I am talking about. They were getting well into the wine, too, which was really, really unusual for Crippen. He is not a drinker, and never has been.

"Then the whispers started among our group: 'Do you see what she's wearing? That is Belle's brooch.' And we were damned sure it really was Belle's brooch; a big sunburst thing, all diamonds and pearls. My wife spotted it first and she and the other women had no doubt about it. A couple of people said the typist's fur might very well have been Belle's, too.

"So there was a very big question: If Belle had gone to the States, why had she not taken her brooch and fur? She loved her jewellery, and it would not be like her to leave any behind.

"One of our group, Louise Smythson, right in front of the typist, asked Crippen if he had heard from Belle. Yes, he had. Then can we have her address? Oh, she is travelling directly to California. Well, what about her address there? Oh, she does not have one yet; she will be up in the mountains. Could we reach her through your son in California? No, she will not be seeing him yet, if at all, and is going straight to the mountains.

22

"Now, I can understand a man having an affair with his typist. I am not a prude. But flaunting it in front of your wife's friends is bad. Having your mistress wear your wife's jewels as if they were hers like that is obviously bad. And not having a realistic explanation as to why those friends have not heard from her in almost three weeks is worrisome, to say the least.

"Look, we do know that Belle had a man friend, a performer from Chicago, Bruce Miller, a one-man band act who performed here but had gone back to the States. We did not know if they were more than just friends. Some of us may have suspected it, but it was not something we talked about. We vaudeville people may look on these things differently than many, I guess, and we are a forgiving lot.

"We wondered, naturally, if the real reason Belle had gone to the States was to see this Bruce Miller. All right, but you can be pretty sure that if Belle was having an affair with Miller she would have at least dropped hints about it. And if she had headed for home to see him, surely she would have let someone among her friends know.

"So we speculated that if she *had* run away to Chicago to be with this Miller, Crippen might simply be trying to save face with his story about an inheritance and a journey to California.

"All right, but where the hell *was* Belle? And why had she not been in touch with a soul other than Crippen? Why had she not taken that brooch with her? And the fur? If she had sailed to New York, why in the name of heaven had she not tried to get hold of Isabel Ginnett? Surely she would have done at least that before moving on to California.

"Those letters, by the way, now are in the hands of the police.

"Now, my wife and I had to go to the States on business. We left on March 23rd. The very next day, unknown to us, Crippen reported to our friends that his wife had died in California. We got this bad news from Mrs. Ginnett when we arrived in New York. She had no details at all, but then she got a letter from Clara Martinetti and Clara was certainly worried, and wondering about Crippen's story.

23

"While we were still in the States, Clara Martinetti and Louise Smythson of the Ladies' Guild went to see Crippen here in London. He told them that Belle had died of pneumonia, in Los Angeles, at the home of his son Otto.

"Mrs. Ginnett had no address for Otto, so she wrote to the city authorities and asked them if they could find Otto and advise him that we wanted information from him about Belle's passing. She got no reply from the city.

Nash slapped the arm of his chair. "I do not have to tell you that everyone back in London began to question all the things that Crippen had said, and to attempt to check them all.

"Mrs. Martinetti asked Crippen for Otto's address, so that the Guild could send a letter and a wreath for Belle's grave. Crippen then said that she had been cremated, not buried, and that her ashes were coming to London. He suggested that everyone could hold a little ceremony here when they arrived.

"Mrs. Martinetti insisted on having Otto's address, and Crippen finally gave it to her. The women quickly sent a card, and the Guild sent a letter to this Otto.

"His letter in reply was much delayed, and when we got it it, it really fanned the flames of suspicion. Otto Crippen said that Belle had *not* died in Los Angeles but in San Francisco, and *not* at his home or in his presence. Indeed, he said that he had not actually known of her death until he got a letter from Crippen. In that letter, Crippen said that he had somehow, and wrongly, given out that Belle had died at Otto's house.

"Louise Smythson was not in the least satisfied with Crippen's story, and took it upon herself to go to your police at your New Scotland Yard. Could they look into Belle's disappearance, and verify Crippen's story?

"The officer there replied that Belle was fully entitled to disappear and remain *incommunicado* if she so chose. This sort of disappearance happened all the time. And he insisted that he had been given no evidence of any crime or attempted crime. Louise gave him a difficult time, and he finally offered two things: the names of steamship companies so that she could check their passenger manifests, and the advice that

24

Louise try the United States Embassy, which could perhaps help confirm that Belle had died in the States.

"The embassy gave no help itself, but told Louise how to find if a death had been registered in California and left it up to her to do this.

"The Guild did attempt to check the steamship passenger lists but that came to nothing. There was simply no record of any Belle Elmore or Cora Crippen sailing on any steamship. I say it came to nothing, but what it did was to confirm to everyone that Crippen *must* be lying.

"Lil and I sailed for England on June 5th, and when we got back to London we immediately got together with our Guild friends. It was clear that by now nobody believed a single damned word Crippen had said, and equally clear that nobody, and I mean nobody, had heard any word at all from Belle. Not one word, from someone who was a prolific writer of letters and postcards. Nothing from her ship, nothing from whatever port she landed at in the States, nothing en route to California and nothing *from* California.

"And there was something even more significant, sir. Mrs. Martinetti and another Guild member, Annie Stratton, had gone to Crippen's house and questioned him here. They asked on what ship Belle had sailed. He gave them a name for the ship. The women failed to write it down, and could not recall it exactly, but it was a French ship with a name like *La Tourne*, which Crippen said was based in the French port of Le Havre.

"Their investigations pretty well determined that the ship in question must have been the *La Touraine*, from Le Havre, but Belle could not possibly have sailed on her. The *La Touraine* was not in service at the time. Crippen was caught in a gold-plated lie.

"After hearing all this from the Guild ladies, bit by bit, story by story, I went to see Crippen myself on Tuesday June 28th. I offered our condolences, and he began to sob.

"But I also wanted information, and I was damned determined to get it. I was going to keep on at Crippen until he answered my questions. I mean, saving face by saying that his wife had gone to California to deal with legal matters is one thing; if he was embroidering that story by saying that she had then died is quite another. So I had a lot of questions for him. But there was something wrong with his answers, and with everything he said.

"I asked him where Belle had actually died. He replied that it was a town near San Francisco that had a Spanish name. Well, I have lived in the area, so I tossed him some of the Spanish names that I knew: Palo Alto? San Mateo? San Carlos? And, going farther out, Alameda? San Leandro? Vallejo? San Rafael? Modesto? Manteca?

"He said that he thought it might have begun with an A, like Alameda. I suggested Alamo, and he quickly said he thought that, yes, it might indeed be Alamo. The answer hit me, though, as just too quick, and too easy, as an attempt to give me *something* and to make me stop asking questions.

"Well, listen, Mr. Holmes, you would think that a man who has lost his wife in the States would know where it had happened.

"He had told our friends that Belle was cremated in California. He told me he already had her ashes, and that they were locked in his safe. So I asked which crematorium, which funeral parlour, had provided the cremation. They would have sent him a bill, or papers, so he should know the name of the company. He hesitated, and then said there were four such companies in the San Francisco area, but that he could not remember which one.

"'You must have got a certificate with the ashes,' I said. "Could we not find out from that?' He evaded the question, and he insisted that he could not remember the company. Again, you would think that a man whose wife has just been cremated in California, and has received her ashes, would remember the name of the funeral parlour or crematorium.

"I kept on at him, but he was either evasive or slick. I was asking solid questions, and getting hot air in response. That is why I decided to put the story to Superintendent Froest, which I did on Thursday June 30th.

"What do you make of it all, Mr. Holmes?"

My friend has been a silent and concentrated listener throughout Nash's account. Now he nodded, several times, slowly.

"You have given a very clear account. If you were hoping for a verdict from me, however, I regret that I must disappoint you, for I have no real evidence upon which to reach a reasoned conclusion.

"Let me say, however, that Crippen's behaviour has been most peculiar and perhaps significant. To my mind, you certainly did the right thing in planning to report it all to the police. I do believe it may be a matter for New Scotland Yard.

"You see, as I have told Chief Inspector Dew, Crippen's actions demonstrate that he is, somehow, certain that his wife is not going to write to any of her friends, nor is she going to turn up at one of their houses, nor appear at the Music Hall Ladies' Guild office.

"Unless he knows something about his wife and her plans that he has not disclosed to anyone, he seems certain that she will never be heard from again."

Nash broke in. "I sense that you suspect, then, that she may indeed be dead. So do some of us, now."

Mr. Holmes nodded. "It is certainly one possible explanation. There may be others, but I think you were justified indeed in taking this case to Superintendent Froest."

Chapter Four

We did not see Chief Inspector Dew again until breakfast-time on July 9th. He was accompanied by his faithful and favourite detective sergeant, Arthur Mitchell, another policeman well known to Mr. Holmes as a clever, intelligent, and observant devotee of detail, even more dedicated than Dew to the careful writing of traditional police notes in the traditional notebook.

"Mitchell and I went to see this Crippen fellow yesterday," Dew reported. "We had spent several days interviewing Mrs. Crippen's music-hall friends, and decided it was time now to hear Crippen's story. We caught up to him at his office, and he gave us a long statement, all quite voluntary and co-operative.

"It turns out, by the way, that he is a qualified doctor, trained in America, although he has been working here in the patent-medicine business. It also turns out that his wife's real name is neither Cora nor Belle, but Kunigunde Mackamotzki, of Russian, Polish and German extraction. Also known as Cora Turner, and as Cora Marsinger, the name of her American stepfather.

"The story Crippen tells us is that his wife is not dead, but is very much alive. That she had, shall we say, a special relationship, here in London, with an American music-hall artist, one Bruce Miller – a one-man band is his variety act – and that she has gone off to Chicago to be with him. Crippen told her friends that she had died, so that they would stop asking him questions about her disappearance. Obviously, that did not work, right?

"But if you are interested, we might begin with a report first on what we have learnt from the music-hall set."

Mr. Holmes sent down for more coffee, and Dew and Mitchell settled into chairs. Dew began his story. "I shall tell you briefly what we have understood from the Nash couple, even though you have spoken to Mr. Nash yourself. Then Mitchell can report on his meeting with another of the music-hall people, Adelene Harrison. He has not yet been able to give me the details in person.

"Mr. and Mrs. Nash had been in America. They knew Belle Elmore and Crippen quite well, and had often seen them before the Nashes left for the United States on March 23rd, on their professional business. On June 5th, they set sail to return to England, but had already learnt from one of the music-hall people then in New York, Mrs. Fred Ginnett, that their friend Belle Elmore had died.

"On arrival in London, they made quick contact with their music-hall colleagues, and found that *they* just could not believe Crippen's story of his wife's passing. As I say, none of them could believe for a minute that she would have left London without saying goodbye or, indeed, inviting them to her and Crippen's house for a farewell. And they could not believe that Mrs. Crippen would have failed to send them constant letters or postcards, beginning with cards from her ship on which she sailed.

"In fact, they had received nothing but Belle Elmore's letters of resignation in February as treasurer of the Music Hall Ladies Guild. There were two such letters."

"Yes, Mr. Nash provided me with copies."

"Then you know that neither was in Mrs. Crippen's handwriting. The first letter, on February 2nd, carried the initials H. H. C., as a *per procurationem*. We know, then, that he wrote that one.

"The second letter, returning the Guild's cheque book and deposit book, also was not in her hand, but had no *per*

30

procurationem notation nor initials from Crippen. He obviously wrote that one himself, though.

"Mrs. Crippen's friends were, to say the least, puzzled and upset that they had not heard from her in person, so, naturally, they soon questioned Crippen himself. On February 7th, for example, he visited Paul and Clara Martinetti, another music-hall couple. They had been guests of the Crippens, at the Crippens' house, on the night of February 1st. Crippen told them that his wife had gone hastily to America, on the morning after their evening together, as the result of a telegram saying that she had to deal with legal business in California involving an estate.

"On March 20th, Crippen wrote a letter to the Martinettis, reporting that he had had news from his wife that she was dangerously ill with double pneumonia. He nodded at Mitchell, who opened and read from his notebook.

Dear Clara and Paul,

Forgive me for not running in during the week but I have really been so upset by very bad news from Belle that I did not feel equal to talking about anything, and now I have just had a cable saying she is so dangerously ill with double pleuro-pneumonia that I am considering if I had better not go over at once.

I do not want to worry you with my troubles but I felt I must explain why I had not been to see you.

I will try and run in during the week and have a chat.

Hope both of you are well, with love and best wishes.

Yours sincerely,

Peter

Dew shrugged. "Peter is a name or nickname by which the music-hall people know and address him. Where it came from, nobody seems really to know, but probably from his wife.

31

"To continue: On March 24th, Crippen sent a telegram to the Martinettis announcing that his wife had died on March 23rd, and that he would be going away for a week or so.' Mitchell read out.

> 24 MARCH VICTORIA STATION BELLE DIED YESTERDAY AT 6 OCLOCK PLEASE PHONE ANNIE SHALL BE AWAY ABOUT A WEEK PETER

"Annie is Annie Stratton, another music-hall person and a friend of the Crippens," explained Dew, as he picked up the thread again.

"On March 30th, Clara Martinetti and another music-hall lady, Louise Smythson, called on Crippen, who had returned home. He told them that his wife had died in Los Angeles, at the home of Crippen's American son, Otto. That is a son by an earlier marriage. The two women asked for Otto's address, and Crippen gave it to them, somewhat reuctantly."

Dew began to check points off on his fingers.

"First, the music-hall friends wrote to the son. Mrs. Smythson came to New Scotland Yard the next day to ask how we could confirm a death that occurred in Los Angeles. The officer on duty referred her to the American embassy.

"Second, the music-hall people tried to determine when and how Mrs. Crippen had left London. On what ship had she sailed, and when? They could find no record of her sailing on any ship at all, from anywhere. There was no record of her on any passenger list, at least not under the names of Crippen or Elmore.

"Third, now we come to June 28th. Mr. Nash went to see Crippen at his office in New Oxford Street, Albion House. Nash says Crippen was emotional about his wife's death, and sobbed. Then – and this is what made Nash begin to fear for the worst – Crippen changed his story. He said his wife did not die in Los Angeles or in San Francisco, but in a small Spanish or Mexican town near San Francisco.

"Now, Mr. Nash had lived in California for a couple of years, and knows the region well. He asked Crippen in which town Cora had died, and threw out some names of small towns with Spanish names. Was it Alamo, for example? Crippen first said yes, but then said that he really could not remember which town.

"Then Nash asked about her place of burial. Crippen replied that she had been cremated, and that her ashes had been sent to him from America. He now had them in his safe. Nash asked Crippen for the name of the crematorium or funeral director, and Crippen would not or could not give it. Nash asked about the death certificate. Crippen replied vaguely:- 'I think I have got it somewhere'.

"I ask you, Holmes, as Mr. Nash asked me, what husband who has just lost his wife overseas does not know where she died, or was cremated, and does not know where the death certificate is? And why *was* she cremated? As a Roman Catholic, that could not have been her choice, and Crippen, as a convert to that church at her behest, would surely have known that.

"Crippen was asked about the ship on which she had sailed to America. Crippen insisted she left from Le Havre. At one point, he gave them the French name of a ship. This name the friends did not recall accurately, but here is something most suspicious: It seems that Crippen may very well have given to them the name of a ship that, indeed, normally sails from Le Havre to New York. But that vessel was actually out at sea when Mrs. Crippen supposedly boarded it, and was then taken to dry-dock for repairs. She simply could *not* have sailed on it when Crippen said she did.

"Now to Crippen's statement to us: Crippen tells me and Mitchell that, after some of their friends visited the Crippens on the night of January 31st, his wife turned on him on the morning of February 1st, and announced that she was leaving him and was going to America. When he came back from work that day, he says, she was gone. So was some of her clothing and jewellery, but she left considerable amounts behind. That is another ground for concern; her friends say she was so thoroughly obsessive about her jewellery that she would never have left any behind, especially the many expensive pieces that she loved.

"After that, Crippen eventually told her friends that she had died in America. He wore a black arm-band, and used black-edged writing-paper. But his story did not convince them, as you know, and they are still asking questions.

"We met the Ethel Le Neve woman, too, by the way, and we have her statement. She admits to an intimate affair with Crippen, and is in love with him, I would say.

"Crippen invited Mitchell and me to search his house up Camden Town way. That we did, last night, but neither of us saw anything suspicious."

Mitchell broke in, politely. "The one thing that stood out for us was the quantity of clothing and jewellery that she left behind; an awful lot of it. But if she was packing in a rage and a hurry, that might explain it."

Dew now waved an inviting hand at Mitchell. "What did you learn from Adelene Harrison?"

Mitchell produced his notebook once more, and began to read from it:- "Interview with Adelene Harrison, with her voluntary agreement, at the Bow Street Police Station, Thursday July 7th, 1912, starting at 2:04 p.m., ending at 3:56 o'clock."

Dew broke in, gently. "Let us get into the written detail a little later. Perhaps you could give us now a general picture of what she had to say."

"Of course, sir. Let me tell you first that Mrs. Harrison is a writer, and has a writer's way with words. She is writing a long tribute to Mrs. Crippen, and is hoping to get it published for the public to read. She not only has a way with words, she has a lot of them. Indeed, she kept quoting words and sentences from her draft article, and was obviously wondering what I thought of them, and whether I was impressed. I let her see that I was. One bit I remember was that Mrs. Crippen was 'a brilliant chattering bird of gorgeous plumage!' I could not stop Mrs. Harrison talking, and could hardly get a question in edgewise.

"Mrs. Harrison is an actress who is married to one Denham Harrison, who, I am told, is a well known writer of songs and a composer."

I interrupted. "He is indeed well known. He wrote *Give Me a Ticket to Heaven*." I started to sing the once-popular tune, until I saw that my audience was unimpressed with the distraction, or perhaps with my limited musical skill.

"The general picture, sir, gentlemen, is that Mrs. Harrison and Mrs. Crippen have been the very best of close friends, for a good 12 years. They have had no secrets from each other, including intimate secrets. However, they had not seen much of each other of late. They may have had a disagreement of some kind, it seems, but Mrs. Harrison would not discuss it. She would say no more than it was a personal matter.

"She did, though, talk at very great length about the relationship between Crippen and his wife, at least as Mrs. Harrison saw it.

"To keep a very long story short, Mrs. Crippen not only wore the trousers in the household, she wore the shirt, shoes, stockings, gloves, and the hat and feathers as well.

"By Mrs. Harrison's account, Crippen did not get much chance to play even second fiddle; his role in the marriage was to do what he was told, when he was told, as he was told, and to pay for everything. And, according to Mrs. Harrison, he was content to do just that. She says that Crippen doted on his wife, and went to extraordinary lengths to keep her happy and supplied with expensive jewellery and clothes."

"Mrs. Harrison said that she has written a number of sketches and plays for Mrs. Crippen. Mrs. Crippen had high hopes of becoming a famous opera singer, but it seems she really did not have that degree of talent, and instead she took to performing sketches in music halls and the occasional smoking concert.

"Mrs. Harrison says that Crippen had appointed himself as manager of his wife's musical career, and that he was dismissed for this by his American employer, James Munyon, a wealthy maker of patent medical cures. Munyon apparently thought Crippen was supposed to be working full-time for

Munyon, with a most generous salary, and not working for himself at the same time as the manager of an artist, even if she was his wife.

"Mrs. Harrison told me that after he was given the sack by this Munyon fellow, Crippen made a bad investment or two and was running a bit short of money. Mrs. Crippen was worried about money, and so was Crippen.

"The story that Mrs. Harrison tells is that Crippen was madly in love with his wife, at least to begin with, and spent a large portion of his income on clothes and jewels for her. However, Mrs. Harrison did agree, when I pushed her a bit, that Crippen might well have drifted away from his wife, as she could be a most overbearing and bossy person, especially if Crippen was short of funds. That was the message, if not in Mrs. Harrison's exact words. She was loathe to be critical about her friend.

"Still, Mrs. Harrison did tell me, if a bit reluctantly, that Mrs. Crippen had frequently belittled Crippen in front of others. Again, when I pushed her, Mrs. Harrison finally said that Mrs. Crippen is a very good friend, but must be difficult to live with as a wife, and that if Crippen had strayed it would be, well, perhaps understandable."

Dew nodded approval. "Good, Mitchell, well done. And that, Holmes, pretty well sums up what we have learnt from the music-hall people about the domestic relationship of the Crippens as a couple."

Dew now picked up his own story again.

"Mitchell and I parted on good terms with Crippen after taking his statement. I told him that I would have to track down Mrs. Crippen, if only to clear the matter up. Crippen asked if it would help if he placed an advertisement for her in some American newspapers. I said that it certainly could not hurt, and he promised that he would place such an advertisement. Speaking of advertisements, by the way, Crippen confirms that it was he who placed the Belle Elmore death notice in *The Era* of March 26th.

Mr. Holmes nodded: "I suppose you will at some stage want to track down this Bruce Miller, by way of the Chicago police? I have useful friends with the Pinkerton National Detective Agency in America, should you have need of their assistance."

"I shall have to go through the official channels," returned Dew. "That should not be too difficult, though,"

Dew shook his head. "I would have thought that, in music-hall circles, Crippen could simply have explained that his wife had left him for another man, rather than all this lying about her illness and death. He seems like a pleasant enough little fellow, by the way. He was quite open about his affair, and he talked freely about his wife and their lack of love for each other. He said they have not shared a bed for four years.

"Hen-pecked he was. At one point, the music-hall people say, the Crippens took in some young German lodgers. Mrs. Crippen required her husband to prepare and serve their breakfasts, make their beds, and even to clean their boots. Hen-pecked? Sounds to me more like hen-persecuted.

"But I have a special exhibit here for you, Holmes."

Dew opened his briefcase, and handed a document to Mr. Holmes. "Here is Crippen's signed statement to us. It is the original, so please handle it very carefully."

Mr. Holmes did so, and then handed it to me. Handling it most delicately, before returning it to Dew, I read:-

Albion House,
61 New Oxford Street,

8ᵗʰ July, 1910.

Hawley Harvey Crippen states: I am forty-eight years of age. After being questioned by Chief Inspector Dew as to the statements made by me that my wife, known as Belle Elmore, is dead, I desire to make a voluntary statement to clear the whole matter up.

I was born at Cold Water, Michigan, U.S.A., in the year 1862, my father's name being Myron Augustus Crippen, a dry goods merchant. My mother's name was Andresse Crippen, née Skinner. My mother is now dead, but my father lives at Los Angeles, California. I was educated first at Cold Water, Indiana, and California, and then attended the University at Michigan until I was about twenty, and finished my education at the Hospital College at Cleveland, where I took the degree of M.D.

I came over to England in 1883, and attended various hospitals to see the operations, and returned to the States, and was assistant for three or four months to Dr. Porter, of Detroit. After that I went to New York and took a degree in special eye and ear work at the Ophthalmic Hospital. This would be in 1885.

After that I returned to Detroit, where I remained about two years as assistant to the same doctor. I then went to San Diego, where I practised as an eye and ear specialist for about two years. Before going to this place I was married to a lady named Charlotte Bell, of New York, and she accompanied me to San Diego.

We then came to New York. I have had only one child by my first wife. He was born at San Diego about 1887 or 1888, and his name is Otto Hawley Crippen. He is now married and lives at Los Angeles.

My first wife died, so far as I can remember, in 1890 or 1891. We were living at Salt Lake City, where I was practising as an eye and ear specialist. She was buried at Salt Lake in my name. After this my son went to live with his grandmother, my mother, until she died. I then went to New York, and went as an assistant to Dr. Jeffery, of Brooklyn, and I lived with him.

About 1893, while with Dr. Jeffery, I met Belle Elmore, who was being attended by him. Her name at that time was Cora Turner. I forget where she was living, but she was living alone. She was only about seventeen years of age, and I, of course, was about thirty.

She, at this time, was living under the protection of a man named C. C. Lincoln, a stove manufacturer, of Water Street, New York. She had been living with him, but he had given up his house and had taken a room for her and was paying all her expenses.

I took her to several places for some weeks, as I was very fond of her, and one day she told me Lincoln wanted her to go away with him. I told her I could not stand that, and would marry her right away, and a few days after this I married her at a minister's house at Jersey City. I forget his name and the name of the street.

I had been married to her some little time when she told me her name was not Turner, but Kunigunde Mackamotzki. She said her mother had been married twice, and her name then was Marsinger, and she was living in Brooklyn. Her mother had been dead some years. My wife told me her father was a Russian Pole and her mother was a German. Her stepfather, so far as I know, is still living, and resides at Forrest Avenue, Brooklyn. Her parents were in rather ordinary circumstances, but she had a good education, and spoke German well.

After getting married to her we went to St. Louis, where I practised as consulting physician to an optician in, I think, Olive Street. His name was Hirsch, I think.

We stayed there about a year, and we returned to New York, where I took a position as consulting physician to the Munyon Company. We lived in the office at East Fourteenth Street.

I was in New York for only a few months when the company transferred me to Philadelphia. I was there with my wife about a year, and was then transferred to the firm's place at Toronto, where I managed their business. I forget where I lived, but we were there only six months, and then returned to Philadelphia.

I was there some time, and while there, about 1899, my wife, who had a good voice, went to New York to have her voice trained, as she thought of going in for grand opera.

I paid all her expenses, and occasionally visited her at New York, and then in about 1900 I came to England alone, where I was manager for Munyon's at their offices in Shaftesbury Avenue, and I lived at Queen's Road, St. John's Wood.

It was in April I came over, and she joined me in August, as she wrote and told me she was giving up her lessons in grand opera, and was going in for music hall sketches. To this. I objected, and told her to come over here. She came, and we went to live at South Crescent.

When she came to England she decided to give sketches on the music -hall stage, and adopted the name of 'Macka Motzki' but she did not make anything at it. She gave a sketch at the Old Marylebone Music Hall, but it was a failure, and she gave it up.

After this she did not do anything in it for two or three years, until I had to go to America about two years after coming here. My firm sent for me, and I became manager in Philadelphia.

When I left England my wife and I were living at, I think, 62 Guildford Street, and she remained there while I was away. I remained in Philadelphia from November till the following June, and sent my wife money regularly.

When I returned I found she had been singing at smoking concerts for payment, and that an American music hall artiste, named Bruce Miller, had been a frequent visitor at her house. She told me that this man visited her, had taken her about, and was very fond of her, also she was fond of him.

I may say that when she came to England from America her manner towards me was entirely changed, and she had cultivated a most ungovernable temper, and seemed to think I was not good enough for her, and boasted of the men of good position travelling on the boat who had made a fuss of her, and, indeed, some of these visited her at South Crescent, but I do not know their names. I never saw the man Bruce Miller, but he used to call when I was out, and used to take her out in the evenings.

When I returned to this country, I did not take up my position at Munyon's, but went as manager to the Sovereign Remedy Company, 13 Newman Street. They failed about eight months afterwards, and I then went as physician to the Drouet Institute, Regent's Park, and afterwards at 10 Marble Arch, and they also failed. From there I took a position with the Aural Clinic Company, 102 New Oxford Street, where I remained until they failed in about six months. I then went back to Munyon's, 272 Oxford Circus, as manager and advertising manager.

I removed to Albion House as manager about eighteen months ago, after which I took it on as an agency, but, as it did not pay, I, in February last, handed it over to the company again, but for the last two years I had been running the Yale Tooth Specialist Company, with Dr. Rylance as partner, and am still doing so.

I ran what I termed the Imperial Press Agency, in connection with Munyon's, because by so doing I got their advertisements inserted at a reduction. At the present time I am interested in an ear-cure business, called the Aural Remedy, at Craven House, Kingsway, and I work at an address in Vine Street.

I did not think anything of Bruce Miller's visiting my wife at the time.

After returning from America we went to live at 34 Store Street for about a year. During this time she adopted the stage name of Belle Elmore, although she had had it in her mind when she came over, but I persuaded her to use the other name.

She got an engagement at the Town Hall, Teddington, to sing, and then from time to time she got engagements at music halls. She went to the Oxford as a comedienne, and was there about a week.

41

She also went to the Camberwell, and also at a hall at Balham. She also sang at the Empire, Northampton, and various towns. She would probably go away for about two weeks and return for about six weeks, but used to earn very little.

We remained at 34, Store Street for some time, and went to 37 the same street for about two years, and about five years ago, in, I think, 1905, removed to 39, Hilldrop Crescent, for which I pay £50 a year.

It is quite four years since she ever went out at all to sing, and, although we apparently lived very happily together, as a matter of fact there were very frequent occasions when she got into most violent tempers, and often threatened she would leave me, saying she had a man she could go to, and she would end it all. I have seen letters from Bruce Miller to her, which ended with 'love and kisses to Brown Eyes'.

About four years, ago, in consequence of these frequent outbursts, I discontinued sleeping with her, and have never cohabited with her since.

She did all the housework herself, with the exception of having a charwoman in occasionally.

About two years ago she became honorary treasurer of the Music Hall Ladies' Guild, and was there every Wednesday. I never interfered with her movements in any way; she went in and out just as she liked, and did what she liked; it was of no interest to me.

As I say, she frequently threatened to leave me, and said that if she did she would go right out of my life, and I should never see or hear from her again.

On the Monday night, the day before I wrote the letter to the Guild resigning her position as treasurer, Mr. and Mrs. Paul Martinetti came to our place to dinner, and during the evening Mr. Martinetti wanted to go to the lavatory. As he had been to our house several times, I did not take the trouble to go and show him where it was. After they had left, my wife blamed me for not taking him to the lavatory, and abused me, and said, 'This is the finish of it. I won't stand it any longer. I shall leave you tomorrow, and you will never hear of me again.'

She had said this so often that I did not take much notice of it, but she did say one thing which she had never said before, viz., that I was to arrange to cover up any scandal with our mutual friends and the Guild the best way I could.

Before this she had told me frequently that the man she would go to was better able to support her than I was.

I came to business the next morning, and when I went home between five and six p.m. I found she had gone. I realised that she had gone, and I sat down to think it over as to how to cover up her absence without any scandal.

I think the same night, or the next morning (Wednesday) I wrote a letter to the Guild saying she had gone away, which I also told several people. I afterwards realised that this would not be a sufficient explanation for her not coming back, and later on I told people that she was ill with bronchitis and pneumonia, and afterwards I told them she was dead from this ailment. I told them she died in California, but I have no recollection of telling any one exactly where she died.

Someone afterwards asked me where my son lived, and I told them. I then put an advertisement in the Era that she was dead, as I thought this would prevent people asking a lot of questions.

Whatever I have said to other people in regard to her death is absolutely wrong, and I am giving this as an explanation. So far as I know, she did not die, but is still alive.

It is not true that she went away on legal business for me, or to see any relations in America.

I did not receive any cables to say that she was ill, and it is not true that she was cremated at San Francisco, and that the ashes were sent to me, or that she sailed from Havre.

So far as I know, she has no claim to any title. I have no recollection of telling any one my son was with her when she died.

We had a joint account at the Charing Cross Bank, subject to the signature of either, but it pleased her to think she was signing cheques, and she also did so, and several blank cheques were always already signed by her, and some of them have been changed by me since her departure, and there is one here now (produced).

When my wife went away I cannot say if she took anything with her or not, but I believe there is a theatrical travelling basket missing, and she might have taken this with

some clothes. She took some of her jewellery, I know, with her, but she left four rings behind, three single stone (or solitaire) diamonds, and one of four diamonds and a ruby, also a diamond brooch. She had other jewellery, and must have taken that with her. I have never pawned or sold anything belonging to her before or after she left.

Everything I have told you is true.

I do not know what clothes, if any, she took away; she had plenty. Whenever we quarrelled, and she threatened to leave me, she told me she wanted nothing from me. I have bought all her jewellery, and, so far as I know, she never had any jewellery presents, and I do not know that she ever had any money sent her, except that Bruce Miller used to send her small amounts on her birthday and at Easter and Christmas, to purchase a present.

She suffered from bilious attacks, and I have given her medicine for that, homoeopathic remedies.

It is true that I was at the Benevolent Fund dinner at the Criterion with Miss Le Neve, and she wore the brooch my wife left behind. She has also worn my wife's furs.

Miss Le Neve has been in my employ, and known to me through being employed by the firms I have worked for, for the past eight years, and she is now living with me as my wife at Hilldrop Crescent. I have been intimate with her during the past three years, and have frequently stayed with her at hotels, but was never from home at nights.

After I told people my wife was dead Miss Le Neve and I went to Dieppe for about five days, and stayed at a hotel there (I forget the name, but the proprietor's name was Vacher) in the names of Mr. and Mrs. Crippen.

My belief is that my wife has gone to Chicago to join Bruce Miller, whose business on the music hall stage is a musical instrument turn, but I think he has now gone into another business, and has speculated and made money. Mr. Didcot was his agent when he was over here.

I shall, of course, do all I can to get in touch with her, so as to clear this matter up.

She has a sister named Louise, whose name is Mills, living with her husband, who is a soapmaker living at Brooklyn. They live with my wife's stepfather, Mr. Marsinger. I do not know where any of her other relations live. I cannot tell you how you can find or trace her, except as I have already said.

I will willingly go to my house with you to see if I can find any letter which may throw any light on the matter, and I invite you to look round the house, and do whatever you like in the house.

This is all I can tell you. Any notes that I have changed through any one in this building were in connection with my business.

This statement has been read over to me. It is quite correct, and has been made by me quite voluntarily, and without any promise or threat having been held out to me.

Hawley Harvey Crippen

Mr. Holmes spoke first. "He has covered a lot of ground there. How genuine do you see it? Did it come across to you as truthful, or, rather, as prepared and rehearsed."

Detective Sergeant Mitchell shook his head. "I was so busy writing all this down that I did not have much chance to study him. But when you asked if he sounded prepared and rehearsed, I think you may have it. He seemed to have anticipated a lot of our questions and had got his answers down pat."

Dew was silent for a few seconds. "I really don't know. He had answers to all our questions, but was he prepared and rehearsed? Well, I have to say that he *sounded* truthful to me. But ..."

"But a liar, one way or the other," Mr. Holmes observed. "If he lied to her friends, did he lie to you? And I know you and Mitchell of old, Dew: You are not going to rest until you have determined the truth. Do, please, let us know what you find."

"That I shall," promised Dew. Mitchell nodded agreement.

The next day, Sunday July 10th, Dew and Mitchell sent to Mr. Holmes an urgent telegram, then hastened to meet him at Baker Street, almost beating the telegraph boy.

"Gone," was the first word Dew said, on his brisk entry. "Vanished. Disappeared. Off and away. Crippen has gone. So has Le Neve; presumably together. On the ninth, right after we left you fellows here."

"He has fled? He panicked?"

"It seems that he did, or Ethel le Neve did. We had circulated his wife's description as a missing person. Mitchell and I went to see Crippen to follow up with more questions. Just routine stuff, you know, in the case of a missing person. Are there *other* people she knew well and might have gone to? Has she relatives in America, and where do they live? Might she have gone to them? Has she a favourite city to visit? Has she been to any foreign countries in the past? Has she withdrawn money from their bank? Does she have another bank? You know the routine, Holmes. But we did not find him, neither at his office nor at his home.

"At his office, we found out that he had told his colleagues on the ninth that he had to go away 'to escape trouble' and to avoid a scandal. He left the office that afternoon, and we learnt that Miss Le Neve left at the same time."

Mr. Holmes looked serious. "And so you are betting that Crippen has fled as a result of your inquiries. 'The wicked flee when no man pursueth', but in this case a dogged chief inspector pursueth."

Dew smiled. "And a consulting detective with a remarkable nose for crime?"

"If you will continue to put up with me, yes, indeed."

Chapter Five

Dew and Mitchell visited us again, three days later. Dew smiled, grimly.

"Still no sign of Crippen and Le Neve, anywhere, although we have had dozens and dozens of tips. According to the sightings, he and Le Neve have frequently managed to be in several places simultaneously and hundreds of miles apart, and even in several countries, to boot. As well as being seen getting into a hot-air balloon together; I ask you. You know what it is like, and how hard we have to work to investigate and deal with every tip, no matter how vague.

"Now, Holmes, Mitchell and I have searched his house again but we found nothing that would amount to evidence. We now are going to turn it upside down and inside out. Up the chimneys and down the lavatory; the lot. We'll have the floorboards up and the wallpaper off the walls if we need to. We wondered if you would care to accompany us? Purely unofficially, of course. Mitchell and I would personally be most grateful if you would assist, but the idea actually came from well above us. Frosty knows that we have talked, and he did say that you have eyes that can not only see things, but see through them. Sir Melville has agreed."

Mr. Holmes look surprised. "Sir Melville? Macnaghten? The assistant commissioner himself?"

Dew shrugged. "All that Sir Melville would say was that he is heavily indebted to you for your work on some very special case. He would not give up a single clue or hint, but did say that you saved the Yard's bacon. Open up, now, what was it?"

"Ah, that I cannot tell even you, Dew; you will understand, I hope. But, good heavens; what a most unexpected endorsement from Sir Melville. I shall of course take it to be fully confidential, and thus never to have occurred. But how can I say no? To him, or to you?"

We thus went now to Crippen's rented house: 39, Hilldrop Crescent, off the Camden Road, between Holloway and Camden Town. Just a stone's throw from the Holloway Prison for Women, and not far from Pentonville Prison, as Mr. Holmes pointed out. Number 39 was a semi-detached house on a leafy street; a most ordinary house on a most ordinary street, that nobody would look at twice in passing. Dew led us in, and sent the constable on guard duty off for a break.

The house was untidy, stuffy, and none too clean. The main floor was redolent of damp, and the lower floor that accommodated the kitchen and a breakfast room, and a small, narrow coal cellar under the front steps, was cluttered, gloomy, damp, and dirty. With Dew's permission, I opened some windows to let in fresh air, and became even more aware of strange, persistent noises from somewhere in the neighbourhood.

"What on earth is that racket?"

Detective Sergeant Mitchell smiled. "The cattle market, sir. The new Smithfield. Cattle, pigs, sheep, goats. Animals for sale, and their meats; and the slaughterhouses; all just a few streets away."

Dew gave us a tour of the house.

In one bedroom, he pointed to a framed photograph of a man: "That is Bruce Miller, the one-man band. Crippen says that Miller wrote letters to Cora Crippen and signed them 'with love and kisses to Brown Eyes'."

In another room, Drew held out to us a piece of paper. "Look at this, the advertisement that Crippen drew up to place in the American newspapers. We found it under the sofa."

Mr. Holmes took the piece of paper. "'Mackamotzki: Will Belle Elmore communicate with H. H. C., or authorities at once. Serious trouble through your absence. 25 dollars reward ... *etcetera*'. Dollars, of course. That would be, what, some five pounds two and six, I think. But he apparently did not place the advertisement. Why not?"

The furniture and furnishings were cheap. Pink was a predominant colour – enough to make me wince – in wallpaper, paint, lampshades, knick-knacks, and more, presumably reflecting Cora Crippen's preference. There were even ghastly pink bows and ribbons attached to the corners of some of the framed pictures.

"Hardly a palace," observed Drew, as he showed us each room, and the contents he and Mitchell had found there.

"The queen of the palace upon her departure left a remarkable amount of her possessions behind," observed Mr. Holmes. "Much clothing, as Sergeant Mitchell has noted, and mountains upon mountains of what I take to be her stage costumes. Dozens and dozens of ostrich feathers; quite enough to make a new bird or two.

"Now, we are to believe that Mrs. Crippen left for America in February, in winter, but left her furs behind?"

Dew winced. "I saw the furs but I missed the connection with an American winter, I must confess. One to you."

"And she left behind all this jewellery, as well, Dew? In my limited experience, a woman's jewellery is the very last thing she will fail to take. This was a sudden departure indeed, giving her no time to pack with careful thought. Or ..."

"Or the story of her voluntary departure has a large hole in it," offered Dew.

The garden behind the house looked well cared-for. "Crippen was something of a gardener, we are told," said Dew. Mr. Holmes pointed to a well used tarpaulin, covered with a litter of branches and sticks, and some old flower pots. He lifted a corner. Beneath the old tarpaulin was a heap of earth.

"Nothing there," said Dew. "I took a poke or two at that, with that spade. Mitchell and I have dug up several beds and spots that were not covered in lawn. We found nothing. We even moved that little greenhouse there to see if anything was buried under it; no luck."

Holmes heaved the tarpaulin aside, and went into action with the spade himself. After some furious digging, he looked grimly at Dew.

"Look, Dew. The top layer of the pile is this: good, friable garden soil." He picked up a handful of the dark earth, showed it to Dew and Mitchell, and let it fall through his fingers. "But under it we have a thick layer of clay. And under that layer of clay I see yet more perfectly good garden soil.

"Now, I can understand keeping the good soil for future use in the garden. But why keep clay? I am no gardener, but why would anybody dump a pile of clay on a stock of good soil, then cover it up with more good soil, and protect both with a tarpaulin? And with all that litter? Was the intent to hide the clay? Why is it here? Where did it come from? Why was it dug up? And did something replace it where it was dug up?"

Dew and Mitchell stood in silent puzzlement. Then Dew burst out:- "The cellar. The little coal cellar in the basement. Brick floor, probably just set in clay."

The four of us ran into the house. The cellar floor under the front steps was indeed brick, covered with coal dust. There was a small pile of coal to one side, some branches and firewood, and *detritus* that included an old chandelier. The floor appeared never to have been disturbed, but Dew began to scrabble at it with his hands. "Mitchell, please get the spade, or the poker."

In went the poker, between two bricks, and one brick came partially loose from its clay bed. Dew and Mitchell worked away hard together, and loosened and raised more bricks. Mitchell then ran to the garden to get the spade.

Dew began to dig at the heavy clay. After his spade had cleared a small area, going down six inches or so, a foul smell hit us. A horrid stench that I knew from my army service in

India and my own medical practice; the stink of rotting meat, decaying flesh.

We literally ran for the outside, and gulped its fresh air. Dew dispatched Sergeant Mitchell, on the run, to fetch constables from the local police station. Mitchell soon returned with Constables Daniel Gooch and Frederick Martin, and two more spades. The policemen removed their jackets and re-entered the little cellar. Mr. Holmes and I, standing back a little so as not to interfere with the digging in the cramped space, but able to watch, lit pipes. Dew and Mitchell lit cigars. One old police technique of dealing with such a stench is to burn coffee grounds in a frying pan on the stove, but, even if coffee was available, the grimy kitchen was too far from the cellar for such a trick to work. Tobacco smoke would have to do.

Constables Gooch and Martin gagged, until Mitchell gave them the last cigars from his pocket-case. The digging began again, and it soon became clear what we had found: a shallow grave or pit, measuring some four feet long and somewhat less than two feet across. It was hard at first to determine if the buried remains in it were animal or human. The excavation also contained what looked like lime, some of it in rock-like lumps. The remains themselves were jumbled together in a messy heap.

"Well, Doctor," said Dew through the handkerchief he was holding over his nose. "Is this what I think it is?"

I rolled up my sleeves, reluctantly, and gingerly lifted apart some of the remains and then separated more, and I soon gasped aloud in horror.

"My God, Dew. It is human flesh, I am sure, but he or she has been butchered and filleted. No arms or legs. No head. It is just flesh here; a torso that has no bones in it. I see heart and liver, and so on but no organs, or the pelvis, that would enable me to determine the gender. It is just flesh, carved from the body. The victim has been dismembered, mutilated and, I swear, filleted. My God, this is bloody savagery."

Then I pointed to a small metal object in the pit. "Dew, that seems to be a curler; a hair curler. So …"

"A woman," said Dew. "It is she. It is Mrs. Crippen. It must be."

I pointed again. "And those are surely the remains of a female combination undergarment."

"Look, Dew," broke in Mr. Holmes. "Dr. Watson should do no more. You must send for the divisional police surgeon. Kentish Town? Dr. Marshall?"

"Yes, you are quite right. I am afraid that I must take full command now, and ask you both to leave here. You indeed have eyes that can see through things, but you cannot stay here in the cellar any longer. This is a police case now, and almost certainly a murder case. I shall expect you to be available at Baker Street in case I need to send for you. I shall have to take statements from you both, of course.

"For now, I must secure the premises, and nobody must be allowed in here until Dr. Marshall gets here. What is it, five o'clock? I will enter that in my notes, and I must write it all up. I must find a telephone somewhere and get word to Superintendent Froest and Sir Melville with all speed.

"Mitchell, will you please do your best to get Dr. Marshall here as fast as you and he can manage? And more constables. Gooch, Martin, you will stand guard here; one of you outside the cellar here and the other guarding the front hall above. When more constables arrive, ensure that one will stand guard on the front steps, and another at the tradesmen's entrance. And first lock all the outside doors. Nobody must be able to get into the house without my say-so."

Mr. Holmes and I were still near the house, some 20 minutes later, attempting to summon a cab on Camden Road, when we saw Assistant Commissioner Macnaghten speed into Hilldrop Crescent in his motor, accompanied by Superintendent Froest. He was followed moments later by a panting Mitchell and Dr. Marshall, on foot.

"Greetings, Holmes," cried Marshall. "Detective Sergeant Mitchell told me that you and your colleague were here. I am glad that you did not get too far away. Dr. Watson, is it not? I am Tommy Marshall, the divisional police surgeon. You

54

fellows had better come back to the house with me, and wait in the drawing room or somewhere until I call for you."

Macnaghten reiterated those instructions at the house, and the pair of us sat in stunned silence in a pink-painted sitting room for almost an hour. Dr. Marshall then summoned me, leaving Holmes alone in the ghastly pink room.

"Dew and I are going to ask you to describe and demonstrate what you did to the remains," Marshall explained. "Dew and Mitchell will be taking notes, and Sir Melville will observe, so you must be accurate in your statements." I nodded agreement, and down we went to the cellar. The stench and the remains were still there, but the cellar also reeked of tobacco smoke.

The remains now were fully exposed. Constables Gooch and Martin had been carefully digging, under Dew's supervision. Sir Melville nodded at me. "Dr. Watson? Would you care for a cigar? I brought some with me for the lads. I knew what to expect in the way of stink."

Dr. Marshall questioned me about what I had touched and done with the remains, then nodded comfortingly. "I think all is well, doctor. You have done nothing to which I would object. I needed to know in detail about the condition of the body before, during and after your presence. Now, we must talk to Mr. Holmes. Dew, I suggest that you and your men finish digging around the body and try to see if there is anything under it. Be very, very careful, though, not to damage it with your spades."

Marshall, Froest and Sir Melville joined us in the ugly pink sitting room. Holmes explained that he had not touched the body himself, nor moved anything.

"But you miss nothing, Holmes," said Sir Melville. "Your observations and opinions, please."

Holmes nodded, and began: "We have mutilated remains that both Dr. Watson and I judge to be human. We also have, I observed, a curler with a length of hair caught in it, dark brown, but, I think, partially bleached; although that could perhaps be due to the action of lime in the grave. I also noted what appeared to be underclothing, a woman's underclothing, as Dr. Watson suggested. It had pearl-like buttons, six visible, with one of them fastened. There was a piece of material that looked like a knotted handkerchief. There were also pieces of what I took to be a flannelette pyjama jacket. It was tattered and rotted, but bore a label: 'Shirt-makers, Jones Brothers (Holloway) Limited, Holloway, N'. The jacket is striped in pattern; the colours difficult accurately to determine because of the very poor light in the cellar, but I incline to dull brown and green stripes."

Dr. Marshall and the assistant commissioner took notes as Holmes spoke, then Sir Melville had him describe his actions in the cellar. "And you are sure, Holmes, that you yourself at no time touched, moved or disturbed the remains?"

"I am quite sure of that. I merely observed."

"And your thoughts, Holmes?"

"I shall assume for the moment that this is the victim of murder, and of a strangely unique and poorly executed attempt to conceal the body."

"Strange?"

"Why dismember and gut the body? Why remove the head, limbs, bones, and, it seems, the genital organs? Surely that was to defeat attempts to identify it. But, in that case, why remove all the bones? Why dissect the flesh from the skeleton, and then remove the skeleton? If you have dismembered and dissected the corpse, you now have to dispose of the head, the limbs, all two hundred and six bones and so on. Not so easy, I would say. And why this laborious method? Why go to such lengths to conceal the *identity* of the body rather than simply hide the *whole* body? Why not stuff the corpse into a trunk and drop it off a steamer in the river? Or in the Channel? Or bury it somewhere?"

"You also say 'poorly executed', Holmes. Why so?"

"The lime, Sir Melville. The murderer used generous quantities of lime in the assumption that it would destroy the buried flesh. But quicklime is in my experience more likely to preserve a body than to eat it away, as I am sure Dr. Marshall can confirm. Judging by the condition of the lime in the grave, perhaps natural dampness slaked the lime. That would produce intense heat, true, but in fact that would more likely dessicate and preserve flesh than destroy it. Slaked or unslaked, the use of lime was a mistake. One murderer, Henry Wainwright in 1874, made the same mistake with chlorinated lime. He tried to dispose of his mistress's body with it. Instead, the lime preserved the corpse. He was hanged as a result."

"Would it take medical or surgical experience for a man to dismember and remove all the bones?" inquired Froest. "What say you, Dr. Watson?"

"Not necessarily," I replied. "If you were determined enough, and had the nerve and the time, and had the means of disposing of the detritus, I would say you could indeed do it without medical training. However, it would probably be easier and quicker if you had medical and dissection experience. Indeed, a skilled pathologist accustomed to conducting post-mortem examinations could probably do it all in a matter of an hour. I take it that you ask because of Crippen's medical background?"

"We must not speculate on that," returned Sir Melville. "Let us stick to evidence. For one thing, we do not know how long the body has been buried here. Was it after Crippen's tenancy began? Or has it been here from before that? We do not yet know. And, furthermore, of course, we do not yet know *who* it is, or how he or she died.

"Now, gentlemen, we are ready to release you. We do ask, though, that you do two things: First, say absolutely nothing about this case, to anyone; we would prefer that it not be known that you have been here. Second, please stay in London until further notice, and make yourselves available at our request. We must take signed statements from both of you.

"All that said, Mr. Holmes, your record speaks for itself. May we call upon you if we need further assistance?"

"My heart is ever at your service, my lord."

As all present looked puzzled, including me, Holmes explained:- "A quotation from Shakespeare; Alcibiades in *Timon of Athens*. On a more serious note, this is a most repugnant case, and I shall assist whenever and wherever and however I can."

Chapter Six

Mr. Holmes's unofficial, but officially endorsed, assistance began with him spreading word to his many informants and underworld acquaintances that he would be grateful for any help in finding Crippen, or clues to his whereabouts.

Dew thanked him profusely, when we met him again, in his little office at New Scotland Yard on July 16th.

"Sir Melville proposed that I brief you regularly on our progress in the Crippen case," began Dew. "I am happy to do so. I believe that you will be pleased at our progress, although we have yet to find Crippen and Le Neve."

"You have done the usual? Circulars to railways and shipping companies? Notices at stations, the docks, taxi stands, police stations, post offices, public libraries and so on? Notices to hotels and boarding houses?"

"Oh, yes, all done, and a great deal more as well; but no luck yet."

"I believe that entertainers such as Mrs. Crippen favour certain boarding houses in the provincial cities where they perform. No doubt someone in the trade can identify them for you."

"Good idea; we will certainly pursue that, but you would think that if she were at one of them, her friends would have heard it through their professional grapevine by now."

"Post-watch warrant?"

"Indeed. Under a Home Office Warrant, any letters coming to Crippen's offices and companies, and the home of his long time employee, William Long, are under watch. So is any post coming to the homes of members of Miss Le Neve's family and friends. We are asking the Home Office to expand the warrant to cover telegrams.

"I doubt that Crippen is going to write to any of the music-hall people, but his employee William Long is a distinct possibility. Miss Le Neve may very well write to her family. If she does, the post may help us determine where she is."

Dew now waved at the nearby globe on its ornate stand.

"We have privately notified French and Belgian police. Crippen has visited France more than once, and apparently speaks French quite well, so that seemed advisable. The Foreign Office is going through the formal diplomatic routine of officially notifying them and a host of other foreign authorities.

"Le Neve's father now has told us that Crippen and Le Neve were married, according to her, at least; although when and where is unknown to him. He says that the two have stayed in France several times in small hotels. We have asked him to place an appeal in newspapers for Miss Le Neve to contact us. The father's name is Walter Neave, by the way; a different spelling. That is why we are using Neave, N-e-a-v-e, as an alias for her in the 'Wanted' notice.

"We have also notified some foreign ports, in case Crippen has managed to get away on a steamer. And we have advised the police in a list of American cities with which Crippen had, and may still have, some connection: Let me see: Los Angeles, San Francisco, San Diego, Cleveland, Detroit, St. Louis, Philadelphia, New York, and some others. Oh, and Toronto in Canada as well."

"And Chicago, for Bruce Miller?

"Yes, there too, although we have had no response yet."

'Mrs. Crippen was last seen on February 1st, you said. By whom?"

"Early on Tuesday morning, February 1st, by a music-hall couple, Paul and Clara Martinetti. They had been invited to dinner at the Crippens' house on the evening of Monday, January 31st. They said that it was a pleasant and jolly evening; the four dined and played whist. The Martinettis left at approximately 1:30 in the morning on Tuesday the first. That, as far as we know, is the last time anyone other than Crippen saw Cora Crippen alive. She has certainly made no further contact with any of her friends, which they insist is so unusual as to be simply unbelievable."

"Did anyone see Mrs. Crippen leave the house? Neighbours? Anybody pick her and her luggage up? Taxi? Growler? Motor? Carter? Did she take an omnibus?"

"All checked or being checked and double-checked, but with no result yet. We have gone twice from door to door in the neighbourhood, of course, looking for anyone who saw her after that, but with no success."

"That put the newspapers onto the case, I see."

"That or somebody spoke out of turn, I am afraid. There were people, and some reporters, gathering outside the house even as we dug in the cellar. You must have seen them when you left. The first reports on the finding of the body were printed almost immediately, for heaven's sake."

"Yes, we saw Thursday's *Daily Mail*: 'Mystery of London House, Discovery in a Cellar', and so on. And then yesterday's papers, of course; many more lurid headlines."

"We are already receiving fruitless tips and false leads as a result of the press stories," returned Dew. "Even the American press has been pursuing the story. So we decided upon an unusual move: We invited representatives of the press here to meet with us, and we made a full statement to them and answered their questions.

"But of more importance: I obtained a warrant this morning for the arrests of Crippen and Le Neve, and we have issued a full public notice. That notice is on its way around the world now.

Dew handed to Holmes a copy of the notice, signed by Sir Edward Henry, the police commissioner.

"'MURDER AND MUTILATION'," read Holmes, aloud. "And all in the finest capital letters. You have explained Peter as a nickname that the variety set called Crippen; but what about this other name in here, Franckel, as an alias for Crippen?"

"Franckel, we are told, is another name that he has used, apparently for some company that he owned or managed that treated deafness, or claimed to."

Holmes now asked a most important question. "The notice says that Crippen is wanted for the murder of Cora Crippen. You have formally identified the remains?"

"Well, Holmes, in a definitive sense, we have not. The identity is not actually confirmed yet, nor is the cause of death. Dr. Pepper, who conducted the *post mortem* examination yesterday, confirms that the remains are human, but their identity is still not known for certain. The curler that Dr. Watson pointed out is certainly the same type as that used by Mrs. Crippen, and that partly bleached hair could well be hers. Her hair had been treated in such a way, her friends say. The hair was dark brown at the roots, and with no sign of grey. That could well fit with Mrs. Crippen's age of thirty-seven. The camisole is of a type that she has been known to possess and wear.

"Of more pertinent interest is that Dr. Pepper spotted, on a piece of skin, something that he believes to be the mark of an old surgical scar. We are trying to establish whether Mrs. Crippen ever had an operation that might have left such a scar. Still, we felt that the warrant and notice should not be delayed."

"If there is no word on identity or cause of death," asked Holmes, "do we at least know how long the remains had been in the cellar?"

"Ah, on that we have good news, Holmes. Pepper is sure that the body had been there for some four to eight months, and that it had been buried very shortly after death."

"Here we are in mid-July," observed Holmes. "Mrs. Crippen disappeared six and a half months ago. That falls neatly into Pepper's estimate of four to eight months. Not conclusive, I agree, but of interest."

Dew nodded. "Yes, that struck us, too. What is really significant is that this means that the burial must have taken place well after Crippen had become a tenant in the house. It could not have been buried in his cellar before he moved in. That was in September 1905.

"Now, you will remember Crippen's statement to us. He spoke of his wife frequently seeing this Bruce Miller, here in London, during Crippen's absence on business in America. Crippen added that his wife changed towards him, developed a violent temper, abused him, and thought he was not good enough for her. He says, as you know, that they had not slept together for four years. All that could suggest some motive for murder. Get rid of the wife and settle down with Le Neve."

Mr. Holmes laughed. "No sale! We all know better than to theorise before we have data. Let us not twist the limited facts to suit a theory, but adjust the theory to suit the facts."

Dew nodded in agreement. "So true, and we have so few facts. It is merely his statement to me and Mitchell and therefore indeed of limited value."

"True, but his flight is another fact, and a form of statement, although whether of guilt or of panic we do not yet know. To what extent have you been able to verify the elements of his statement?"

"We have made some progress. By the way, their friends repeat that Mrs. Crippen was the undisputed empress of household, but her friends say Crippen always seemed happy to have it that way."

"Perhaps not surprising, if he had this Ethel Le Neve as a mistress. A pleasant second life to compensate for the defects in the first. What about money?"

"Income on the fair-to-middling side, and all his. But here is something of interest: Their money was held in a joint account at the Charing Cross Bank. During her supposed absence in America, we have confirmed that several cheques bearing her signature were cashed. Crippen admits to cashing them, and says that this was not at all unusual. She had signed blank cheques.

"She brought in no income herself?"

"Not really. She had attempted for some time to become a leading music-hall artiste, as you know. She performed in a number of shows and concerts but her friends admit, with some embarrassment, that her art was somewhat limited. She was not a popular success, appeared in lesser theatres, and earned very little. She certainly depended upon Crippen for money. Her friends say that he was quite generous in that regard, although his income in the last few months was nothing to boast about."

Holmes chuckled and, shook his head. "Yes. For whom did he work? Let me see if I can recall them from his statement to you: Munyon's Remedies, the Drouet Institute for the Deaf, the Sovereign Remedy Company, the Aural Remedy Company and the Yale Tooth Specialist Company. The Drouet Institute is of remarkably doubtful honesty, I have heard. All in all, somewhat less lucrative than a private practice in Harley Street, I imagine."

I could no longer hold my laughter, and let go with a royal belly-laugh. Holmes and Dew looked askance at me.

"Sorry, you fellows, I could not help it. Munyon's Remedies, you see, are well known frauds and quacks who sell patent cures, and are famous for (I burst out laughing again) Munyon's Pile Ointment!"

Mitchell laughed, but Dew ignored me. "The Aural Remedy Company – that should be the Aural Remedies Company, plural, so Crippen signed off on the wrong name there – and the Imperial Press Agency. That last deals with advertising placed in the newspapers and in all the popular weeklies. The Drouet Institute, as you suggest, is known to us as fraudulent from beginning to end, so we must have doubts about these others."

Holmes turned to Dew. "When is the last time that Crippen was seen?"

"At his office at Albion House, on New Oxford Street, at approximately one o'clock in the afternoon of Saturday July 9th. It took two damned days for one of his employees there, William Long, to admit finally that Crippen had got him to go out and buy a boy's suit, hat, shoes in size five, and a tie and braces. Those were presumably for Miss Le Neve; a disguise to flee in. Crippen gave Long two pounds for this, and Long carried out the errand. Then Crippen left, and has not been seen since. Nor has Le Neve. By the way, Albion House is also where the Music Hall Ladies' Guild meets, although in separate rooms."

"You say that you have advised the French and Belgian police. The newspapers there, too?"

"Yes, indeed, and we have sent notices to newspapers in Spain and Sweden and the Canary Islands, in case Crippen has managed to take a steamer."

"Shall you offer a reward?"

"That will be officially announced quite soon. A big one: two hundred and fifty pounds, it will be. In the meantime, we search and hunt and question and wait. And we have to put up with a damned silly ditty that I have heard everywhere:-

> "'They seek them here, they seek them there,
> "'The bobbies seek them everywhere,
> "'Wondering where they've gone trippin',
> "'Ethel Le Neve and Doctor Crippen.'"

I had seen this doggerel already in one of the many newspapers I had searched for stories on Crippen; an easy task given the size and prominence of many of the headlines.

I had learnt from the press, for example, that thousands of people had trekked to Hilldrop Crescent to stare and glare at Number 39, while police stayed outside on guard duty. I read that Cora Crippen was very charming, bright and bonny, beautiful and popular, while Crippen was abrupt and bad-tempered (this description being quite opposite, however, to that given by his friends and his wife's set).

I read of his marriage to Cora in New York. (This was his second marriage, a previous wife, the mother of his son Otto, having died in America in 1892.)

A story in *The Era*, a show-business paper, mentioned in critical tone Crippen's appearance with Le Neve at the Music Hall Ball on February 20th, only nineteen days after Cora's disappearance:-

'It was noticed by the majority of our members, who were somewhat startled, that she was wearing a handsome sealskin coat similar to one which had been worn by the deceased, and even then we did not look so much at her fine clothes as at a beautiful brooch she was wearing, which was exactly like a piece of jewellery worn by Mrs. Crippen. At the dinner the typist sat at his right hand, and later in the evening Mr. Crippen danced with her. It was given out in some quarters that the typist was his wife.'

Reporters spoke to a Mrs. Jackson, Ethel Le Neve's former landlady. She reported that Le Neve had spoken of Crippen divorcing his absent wife, and marrying Ethel. Indeed, Emily Jackson said, Le Neve had shown to her an engagement ring and, later, had brought Crippen to the Jackson house, identified him as her husband, and showed to Mrs. Jackson a wedding ring.

'Miss Le Neve,' added Mrs. Jackson, 'had a gentle, sweet disposition, and I cannot for a moment believe that she had any part in a crime.'

However, Mrs. Jackson had more interesting things to say to our team of detectives. She told us that she suspected that Le Neve had become pregnant by Crippen, and that she had had a miscarriage. Le Neve had not disclosed all this, but the landlady had deduced it. However, she went on to say that Miss Le Neve was an enthusiastic hypochondriac, and so Mrs. Jackson's diagnosis could have been in error.

Holmes looked at it another way. 'If it is true, it could speak to motive for Crippen. Cannot stand his wife, wants to live with his mistress, and now learns that she is pregnant. Time to dispose of Belle Elmore at last. But we need evidence, not theories.'

Le Neve's mother, Mrs. Walter Neave, was quoted in *The News of the World* on the relationship between her daughter and Crippen. 'One day, a week or two before Easter, she suddenly announced to me, 'I'm married, mother! I've married Dr. Crippen!' I was, you may be sure, more than surprised at the news, for I had not even heard of her engagement.'

I was able to point out to Dew and Holmes that, since Easter this year fell on March 25th to 27th, that would place this reported marriage in the range of March 11th to 18th, only six weeks or so after Belle Elmore disappeared.

The story went on to say that Mr. Neave had asked to see the marriage documents 'but she always somehow managed to evade having to produce them'. It was reported that the couple spent some of their supposed honeymoon in Dieppe.

Crippen's partner in business, a dentist named as G. W. Rylance, meanwhile, told *The Pall Mall Gazette* that 'a more humble, unassuming little man I have never met, and to me it seems unthinkable that he would have committed so dastardly a crime'. (*The Gazette* erred; his name was in fact G. M. Rylance.)

I had passed the newspaper stories to Holmes, along with a story from *The New York Times* that our friends at Pinkerton's in America had cabled to us. They sent word, too, that American police were checking all arriving steamers.

Mr. Holmes thanked me, although it was clear that he was not impressed that the journal *Answers* had submitted a sample of Le Neve's writing to a so-called graphologist. My friend's face was quite a study as he read the result:- 'Impulsive, weak-willed, greatly influenced by those who surround her, and much interested in the opposite sex, she is easily attracted, romantic, morbidly sentimental, and allows her heart to entirely govern her head.'

From one of Holmes's many contacts came a really interesting tip. He gave the information to Dew and Mitchell as soon as he received it.

'My informant, Dew, is Ernest Stuart, manager at Attenboroughs, the pawnbrokers, at 142 Oxford Street. They are a reputable firm – no stolen goods – and Mr. Stuart is fully ready to talk to you. His story is this: On February 2nd, the day after Mrs. Crippen disappeared, Crippen took out a loan at Attenboroughs on a diamond ring and a pair of diamond earrings. Stuart gave him eighty pounds, and Crippen signed for it, using his own name and the Hilldrop Crescent address.

'One week later, Crippen returned, this time with six more diamond rings, and a diamond brooch. Stuart advanced one hundred and fifteen pounds on these. He has the jewellery still, and all the documents, and is awaiting your visit.'

"Well done, Holmes. We heard that you have been out fishing for us, and this is a fine catch."

A more valuable catch came to Dew himself, fortuitously, when the inquest (which had opened and quickly adjourned on July 18th) resumed on August 15th.

On July 18th, Dew gave his first evidence about the discovery of the remains, and Dr. Marshall reported on his *post mortem* examination. Marshall said it had not yet been confirmed that the remains were female, but he thought it likely. As is usual in such cases, the coroner adjourned the inquest, until August 15th, to allow police and medical experts to continue their work.

It was on August 15th, then, that Dew happened to walk near Clara Martinetti, one of the music-hall friends of Cora Crippen and perhaps the last of those friends who saw Mrs. Crippen alive. Outside the inquest room, Dew overheard Mrs. Martinetti tell another woman about a serious operation that Mrs. Crippen had undergone.

"I asked her about it immediately, Holmes, and Mrs. Martinetti was quite clear. These were her words:- 'Belle had an operation years ago in America. She had quite a big scar on the lower part of her body. I have seen it'."

Mrs. Martinetti went on to explain that last year, when Mrs. Crippen visited and stayed with her, she had seen Mrs. Crippen undressed. "She had a mark on the lower portion of her stomach, about six inches long. It was an up-and-down mark, a scar from an old cut, I thought. I asked her about it, and she said that she had undergone some surgery."

"You have passed this on to Dr. Marshall?"

"Oh, yes, and to Mr. Pepper. In fact, quite a medical team has been formed. Pepper and Dr. Marshall have been joined by Dr. Willcox and a Dr. Spilsbury."

I knew of 'Wilks' Willcox, the senior analyst at the Home Office, although I had not met him. Spilsbury was a new name to me, but not to Holmes.

"Young Bernard Spilsbury? I know him quite well. An up-and-coming pathologist at St. Mary's Hospital at Paddington. He is rising fast in the field of forensic pathology and has been a most successful workhorse in a number of cases. I have for some time encouraged him to continue in that profession as a career. So have Pepper and Willcox, and so, indeed, has Sir Edward Henry from New Scotland Yard. Does Spilsbury know that Watson and I have been working on this Crippen case? I must get in touch with him.

"Speaking of things pathological, Dew, I take it that you have had no luck finding the head or other body parts? You checked the Regent's Canal, of course?"

"We have dragged the canal in the area, and somewhat beyond, yes, but have found nothing but rubbish, old bicycles, and what-have-you, and several dead animals. No human head or body parts, however. We have checked parks and ponds and woods and copses and other areas as well. We have been over every inch of Hampstead Heath and Highgate Cemetery and Waterlow Park, and The Regent's Park, and Finsbury Park; nothing.

"The waste bins at the slaughterhouses?"

"Oh, yes, of course, we did that right away. No human remains or bones there."

"Railway stations?"

"Yes, Holmes, of course, but there is no sign in any left-luggage office of any trunk or suitcase that smells of decaying flesh or that has leaked any strange fluids. No reports, either, from shipping companies or carters or warehouses of any suspicious crates or packages.

"Now, we do have a dustman who has reported that he removed an unusual amount of rubbish from 39, Hilldrop Crescent from the middle of February until early in March. Some of it, he says, was partly burnt women's clothing. That is of interest, and directs more suspicion at Crippen.

"Of more interest is the dustman's insistence that the rubbish included what he called a strange, light, white ash. We have of course checked Crippen's oven and stove and found nothing unusual. We have done our best to look where the dustman dumped the rubbish, but we have had no luck there."

Holmes nodded, appreciatively. "I would be fairly sure that, if Crippen burnt the head and limbs and bones at his house, the neighbours would have remarked upon the stench."

"Quite right."

"What about Crippen's movements between February 1st and your visit to him on July 8th?"

"Nothing suspicious yet, Holmes. You are wondering about a trip to the country with a big bag of bones and a spade? Under she goes?"

"More likely to the Channel with a big bag of bones and a ferry ticket. Overboard she goes."

"We have come up with no unexplained absences from work, and no record of him leaving London. But he would not have to travel far to dispose of parts of a body. The river, with a weighted suitcase? Dropped from a boat? Or simply from a bridge? It would only take a few hours at night. Burnt? Buried? But where? We have no clues at all in that regard."

"Blood in the house? Fat? Skin? Bone?"

"Chopped her up on the kitchen table, you mean? Dissected her in the bathtub? We thought of all those and more, but there is no sign of such, nor of anything else, come to that. We have examined all the knives in the house, and a hatchet, but found nothing. We have examined all the drains, too, of course, and the sewer, but nothing of interest there. Nothing else buried anywhere in the garden, either."

The two men and Mitchell hammered away at different theories and ideas for a full hour, but reached no conclusions

"Assuming that it is Mrs. Crippen," said Dew, "and assuming that he killed her and carved her up, he has been damned clever about it, and damned devious."

"Not so clever," replied Holmes. "He ran away when you scared him. With Le Neve disguised in that boy's suit, one suspects. A bad move. Not a confession of course, but perhaps it does help to make a case against him."

Dew frowned. "If there is a case to make, Holmes, I am going to make it. You may be sure of that. Now we just have to find the little beggar."

Chapter Seven

Dew again called Crippen a 'little beggar' in his tiny but tidy office at New Scotland Yard late in the evening of Friday July 22nd. He thumped his desk with the palm of his right hand. "Where the hell *is* Crippen; where has the little beggar *gone?*"

A potential answer came fortuitously after another round of New Scotland Yard's strong tea and sugared biscuits. Detective Sergeant Mitchell was called from the room by a constable, and, a moment later, came rushing back in.

"Sir, sir," he cried with a voice that vibrated with urgency and excitement. "It is Crippen, it must be, on a ship for Canada. Here is a telegram from the Liverpool police."

Dew read aloud the telegram, which advised that Crippen was suspected to be on the passenger steamer *Montrose*, bound for Quebec and Montreal from Antwerp in Belgium. The telegram reproduced for Dew the text of a wireless transmission that Captain Henry Kendall of the *Montrose* had sent to his owners in Liverpool:-

MONTROSE. 130 MILES WEST OF LIZARD. HAVE STRONG SUSPICION THAT CRIPPEN LONDON CELLAR MURDERER AND ACCOMPLICE ARE AMONGST SALOON PASSENGERS. MOUSTACHE SHAVED OFF, GROWING BEARD. ACCOMPLICE DRESSED AS BOY, VOICE, MANNER AND BUILD UNDOUBTEDLY A GIRL. KENDALL.

Beaming, Dew looked up. "They obviously have Marconi telegraphy on the ship. What a lucky break. We must get the owners to recall her and bring them home."

"Wait, wait, wait," broke in Holmes. "We do not know if it *is* Crippen. How many false leads have you had already?"

"Dozens upon dozens," responded Dew, honestly.

Holmes nodded. "It would be hard on the passengers, and on the vessel's owners, if we recalled them and then this also turned out to be another false lead. We also do not know if they are still in range for a wireless transmission. Let us try, through the owners, to see if we can get more information by wireless.

"If we fail to make contact, well, if I recall correctly, the *Montrose* is a small, slow ship; an old troopship. Let us determine if there is a faster ship bound for Canada that you or somebody else can catch, and get ahead of him. Imagine being able to greet him as he steps off the *Montrose*, believing himself and Miss Le Neve to be safe."

"Good idea. Mitchell, could you please look into this?

"Sir, it's nearly eight o'clock. The shipping offices will all be closed."

Holmes spoke up. "Could I suggest you call the Liverpool police, Mitchell? They will surely know all about ships from Liverpool to Canada. Ask them if any faster ship is available."

Within twenty minutes, as we waited impatiently, reading and re-reading and debating Captain Kendall's Marconigram, an eager Mitchell returned.

"Sir, there is the *Laurentic*. She is due to leave Liverpool for Quebec tomorrow evening. She's a White Star liner, bigger and newer and definitely faster than the *Montrose*. I am told that she would arrive in Quebec a day or so before the *Montrose* could get there."

Holmes threw in a suggestion:- "You could board the *Montrose* before she even lands at Quebec, perhaps from the pilot boat. That way you would have Crippen all locked up and under guard when the *Montrose* arrives in port."

"A taxi, quickly," Dew instructed Mitchell. "We must get to Sir Melville's house right away."

There, Sir Melville Macnaghten read the telegram from Captain Kendall. "What does your instinct tell you? What do you think?"

"I am willing to bet that it is Crippen and Le Neve, sir," replied Dew. "Captain Kendall seems certain enough. We will try to reach the *Montrose* by wireless, but she would probably well be out of range now. If we fail, may I have your permission to take passage on the *Laurentic*?"

Sir Melville hesitated for a few seconds. "Would it be necessary for you to go yourself? If you were to go yourself, what will happen to the case here? Who will lead it? I suppose that if you go, I must assign another chief inspector."

Dew shook his head. "Sir, I am not sure there is any need for that. Mitchell can lead the case for the moment, with Sergeants Hayman and Crutchett. They are hard at work on it already, and neither has any difficulty at all working under Mitchell. "

Sir Melville looked directly at Holmes. "Holmes, could you continue to be of assistance if Chief Inspector Dew takes the *Laurentic*?"

"Of course, if Chief Inspector Dew and Detective-Sergeant Mitchell can countenance it."

"I would welcome it," returned Dew. "Mitchell would more than approve, too; I know I can speak for him. Mr. Holmes has a knack for keeping us on track and missing no tricks."

"All right," responded Sir Melville. "We will do that. And I am with you, Dew. I think it is very probably Crippen and Le Neve. 'Dressed as boy' is what sold me on it. I will give you written authority right now, along with every blessing and my deepest wish for you to have the best of luck. You can get the Liverpool people to book a ticket for you."

"Duckworth," offered Holmes. "Chief Inspector Robert Duckworth of the Liverpool police. Smart and reliable fellow."

In the morning, through the ship's owners, New Scotland Yard tried again and again to get in touch by wireless with Captain Kendall, but received no response. The *Montrose* must indeed have been out of wireless range, and now could be expected to remain so until close to Quebec.

Thus it was that Dew sailed on the *Laurentic* from Liverpool later that day, Saturday July 23rd, under the name of Dewhurst.

Unfortunately, there was another escape of information to the press, which Scotland Yard then was forced to confirm, and the newspapers of Monday July 25th began to report and speculate on the '3,000-mile ocean race'.

The Daily Mail: 'The drama is being played out between the two ships on the ocean. While Crippen and Miss Le Neve are striving to avoid notice in the *Montrose*, the pursuing vessel *Laurentic* is day by day getting nearer.'

The Daily Telegraph: 'The *Montrose* and the *Laurentic* are both due on the same day, July 30, but it is hoped and believed that the fast boat will pass the Montrose en route, and arrive a few hours in advance.'

Competitive newsboys hoarsely outshouted each other, and there were shouting matches and fisticuffs at newsstands as the public raced to buy the newspapers containing the latest news and speculation. Bookmakers even took wagers on whether Dew would catch up to Crippen.

The Daily Mail on Tuesday July 26th: 'The dramatic chase across the Atlantic of the couple believed to be Dr. Crippen and Miss Le Neve will reach its climax about Sunday .... At noon to-day the *Laurentic* will be only 253 knots (about 283 miles) behind the *Montrose*. The *Montrose* will approximately be in the position of latitude 53 north and longitude 40 west. The *Laurentic* should be in latitude 52 north, longitude 33 west. The *Laurentic* has to make up a leeway of nearly 400 miles in the chase across the Atlantic. A new boat, with a reputation for speed, she ought to be easily able to accomplish the task.' (The landlubber reporter meant 253 'nautical miles', not 'knots', in that second sentence, of course; even I knew that.)

All we could do was to wait.

Sir Melville Macnaghten did not do so patiently. At his pressing invitation, we met in his surprisingly Spartan office at New Scotland Yard.

"With the chief inspector on the high seas, the investigation is designated yours, Mitchell," Macnaghten said with notable formality. "Please bring me up to date on what you have done so far to make the case against Crippen, and what remains to be done."

While a most competent and dogged investigator, Detective Sergeant Mitchell was clearly overwhelmed by the regal presence and influence of the assistant commissioner.

"Well, Sir Melville, we need to press our efforts to establish the identity of the corpse. Is it really Mrs. Crippen? Is any other woman missing? We know of none so far; at least, none with that died hair. And in case it is *not* Crippen on the *Montrose*, we must continue the hunt for him elsewhere and leave no stone unturned."

He stopped, and seemed to be awaiting approval.

"And what else?" asked Sir Melville, patiently.

"Well, sir, we need to know more about Crippen's motive, opportunity, means and inclination and all that, sir. And we need to establish a day-by-day record of Crippen's whereabouts, would you think, Sir Melville? And those of Ethel Le Neve, of course. Could she have been in a position to take part in the murder? Is there any indication that she was a part of it? Or been in a position to know of it? We will have to question her family and friends. Oh, and Mrs. Crippen's movements too, I suppose. Anything else, sir?"

Macnaghten's lips tightened as he said, with just a hint of frustration, "You tell me, Detective Sergeant. What do we do next?"

Mitchell seemed to struggle for an answer, and Sir Melville threw an inviting look at Holmes. "Any thoughts, Mr. Holmes?"

My friend picked up the ball, with a friendly and disarming smile at Mitchell, and let the Sergeant off the hook.

"Well, Sir Melville, I am sure Detective Sergeant Mitchell will develop a most thorough plan. Indeed, he has a reputation for careful planning and execution. One thing that strikes me right off the bat is the need to establish a good and early connection with the doctors so that he can be in on the determination of the cause of death. At this stage, we do not know how Mrs. Crippen – assuming it is her – met her end."

Mitchell interrupted. "We are wondering if she might have been shot, Sir Melville. As our constables went from house to house making inquiries, they have found two women who say that they heard what might have been two shots, somewhere around the end of January or perhaps the early part of February. We have made note of it, of course, but no other neighbour has made a similar report."

Holmes returned to the subject. "So we do not yet know how Mrs. Crippen – if it really is her – came to her death. Shot? Stabbed? Strangled? Beaten? Poisoned?"

At this point, I was able to make a contribution myself that turned out to be important.

"Cream," said I. "Palmer. And the other Holmes."

Mitchell and Macnaghten looked puzzled, but Holmes caught on at once.

"You mean Neill Cream. Thomas Neill Cream."

I nodded, and Holmes, addressing Mitchell, continued. "Cream was a doctor. The Lambeth Poisoner; surely you remember? A Scottish and Canadian doctor, who poisoned victims here and in America, and quite possibly in Canada and Scotland as well. "

"Now I have got it, sir," broke in Mitchell. "He was hanged here in, I think, '92. But what was that about the other Mr. Holmes? And Palmer?"

"*Doctor* Holmes," I interjected. "H. H. Holmes, an American physician and a murderous maniac. We know that he killed at least twenty people, and it may have been five or ten times that number. They hanged him in America in '97. H. H., same initials as Crippen!

"Palmer was earlier, here in England, a doctor who was convicted of murdering a friend with poison. But he may also have poisoned several other people including four of his own children, along with his mother-in-law and his brother. He was hanged many, many years ago."

"Hanged in 1856," added Holmes. "William Palmer, the Rugeley Poisoner. The newspapers called him 'The Prince of Poisoners'. Dickens said he was 'the greatest villain that ever stood in the Old Bailey'. As I have said myself, when a doctor goes wrong, he is the first of criminals. He has nerve, and he has knowledge.

"Excellent thinking there, Watson. You are wondering if Crippen, as a doctor with access to poisons, perhaps poisoned Mrs. Crippen."

"I am indeed, and the medical team will certainly be investigating that. I was struck by the thought that Crippen's office is on New Oxford Street. Also in New Oxford Street is the establishment of Lewis and Burrows, the large chemists. We doctors often order our poisons from them. I suggest that we check with them."

Sir Melville interrupted our review of murderous doctors. "Perhaps, Mr. Holmes, you would help Detective Sergeant Mitchell draw up in writing his a plan of action, and I will ensure that an adequate number of men is made available to execute it. What say you, Mitchell?"

"I would be very grateful, sir, thank you. I believe I have a good plan in mind, but having Mr. Holmes's help and confirmation would be most welcome."

Now, through some of his many continental allies, Holmes also began to trace the movements of Crippen and Le Neve from London to Brussels on July 10th. From photographs of the two, provided by New Scotland Yard, and those circulated by newspapers, the fleeing pair were soon identified as Mr. and Master Robinson.

By way of a ferry from Harwich, and then by train, they first stayed in Brussels at the Hotel des Ardennes, near the railway station. There, we learnt (and the *Daily Mail* reported) that Crippen told the hoteliers (in French) that he was from Quebec and was touring with his son.

The *Daily Mail* quoted the landlady:- 'As the 'father' and 'son' arrived, both looked very tired, the 'son' especially. That 'father' was about fifty, small, and rather bald. He said, in quite decent French, though with a strong English accent, that he was a merchant from Quebec and has just been travelling on the Continent with his son. He took a room on the first floor at 5s a day ....

'After two days, my husband and I agreed that the 'boy of sixteen' was a girl in disguise. 'He' wore girl's shoes and had a girl's figure .... She never spoke aloud all the time we had her here. Her father explained that she was stone deaf, but he was stupid enough to carry on long whispered conversations with her .... Now, we always thought deaf people had to be shouted at.

'Again, it seemed funny that she always had her hands in her pockets. At last one day they dined here and we saw that her hands were beautiful and white, with well-kept nails – a woman's hand quite obviously. We never saw her hair, for she always wore a rather large straw hat which concealed it.

'We called her 'Titine' and nicknamed him 'Old Quebec' because he was always saying, 'My son is ill and must travel. We will go to Rotterdam and thence back to Quebec.' ... We thought him a professor who had eloped with a girl pupil in disguise.'

The two left that hotel on Monday July 18th, and Holmes traced them to a hotel in Antwerp and on to the port of Antwerp.

They were then identified without any hesitation by a shipping agent in Belgium who sold them second-class tickets for the *Montrose*, in the names of John Philo Robinson, aged fifty-five, (Philo, we learnt later, was a name of Crippen's American grandfather) and Master John George Robinson, aged sixteen.

The *Montrose* departed Antwerp for Canada on July 20th. The confirmation that they had indeed booked on the *Montrose* came as great relief to all of us, especially Sir Melville. "So it is them on the Montrose. Thank heaven; I have not sent Dew away on a wild goose-chase. Let us pray that he can get ahead of them."

Holmes also, through the Pinkerton's detective agency, and with the approval of New Scotland Yard, tracked down Bruce Miller, the supposed lover of Mrs. Crippen and now a house agent (I forget the odd American term for it) in Chicago. Miller insisted that he had been only 'the very best of friends' with Mrs. Crippen, and not an *amour*. He knew nothing of her disappearance, he insisted, or her departure from London, and had not seen her since he himself left London in April of 1904.

Pinkerton's also found for Holmes Cora Crippen's younger American sister, Theresa Hunn, and advised that she could confirm in detail that Mrs. Crippen had undergone surgery and could describe her surgical scar. Both she and Miller said they could come to London to testify in person if needed; although Miller said he would insist upon generous payment for loss of his usual income.

A major development came as Holmes and Detective-Sergeant Mitchell followed up on the suggestion that I myself had made. They determined that Crippen indeed had purchased poisons from Messrs. Lewis and Burrows on New Oxford Street.

And the purchase of truly significant note was his acquisition, back on January 19th, of five grains of hydrobromide of hyoscine, a most powerful sedative.

Crippen had told the supplier that this was for five hundred doses of homœopathic medicine (if one may call homœopathy the practice of medicine). It struck Charles Hetherington of Lewis and Burrows as a unique order for Crippen, and a most remarkably large order for anyone, but homœopathy was beyond my ken or interest.

My friend and Sergeant William Hayman investigated Crippen's desk and cupboard at Munyon's Remedies, and a safe to which Munyon's manageress, Marion Curnow, held the key. They found no hyoscine, nor any record of his having prepared homœopathic doses of it. But they did find two envelopes that Crippen had asked her to put away. One included deposit notes from the Charing Cross Bank for six hundred pounds, and the other a watch and brooch. The bank was where Crippen and his wife held a joint account. Mrs. Crippen had written to the bank in December, seeking, without explanation, to close the account and withdraw the whole six hundred pounds, but this required a year's notice.

Speaking of money, the principal of Munyon's, the notorious American quack, J. M. Munyon, so believed in Crippen's innocence that he was to offer an amazing reward of ten thousand pounds to anyone who could demonstrate that Mrs. Crippen was still alive, or could persuade her to come forward to clear her husband. Munyon had employed Crippen in various past capacities, in America, Canada and here in London, for some thirteen years.

Holmes and Sergeant Alfred Crutchett also found a neighbour of Crippen who was sure that on Friday February 4th he had heard a horrifying screech from, he thought, 39 Hilldrop Crescent. This man also insisted that he had smelled burning from the Crippen's garden (immediately behind his own) on the following Sunday, February 6th. Two other neighbours, we already knew, also claimed to have heard screams from Hilldrop Crescent, but on the first or second day of February.

Their statements could not be confirmed, but were carefully noted, and were passed on in full to the Director of Public Prosecutions.

As July came to a close, Holmes and his police colleagues were exhausted.

"I no longer want the old needle," he told me at Baker Street on Sunday July 31st, with a wry smile, and a glance at the mantel-piece where he used to keep his cocaine bottle and his hypodermic needle.

"This case has been more than stimulating. But what I do need, what we all need, is *news*."

Chapter Eight

Then came momentous news indeed: the coup of coups – confirmation of Chief Inspector Dew's successful interception and arrest of Crippen and Le Neve in Quebec.

We were told that cheers echoed and re-echoed throughout a proud New Scotland Yard as a terse telegram from Dew came to its telegraphic address of 'Handcuffs, London' on Sunday July 31st.

> CRIPPEN AND LENEVE ARRESTED. WIRE LATER.

That was soon followed by a second message:-

> CONFIRMING FORMER CABLE. ARREST MADE. ARRIVE QUEBEC MIDNIGHT SUNDAY. SUGGEST MATRON AND MITCHELL. CRIPPEN THREATENED SUICIDE. WRITING SOON. DEW

Our newspapers then gave us endless details of the arrest. They told us how the *Laurentic* had indeed overtaken the *Montrose*, and how Dew had posed as an official St. Lawrence River pilot and had boarded the *Montrose* from the pilot boat. He found Crippen and Le Neve and placed them under arrest.

Some of the stories of the arrest contained details that struck us as fanciful, to say nothing of one newspaper sketch of the arrest that was clearly dreamed up by an imaginative artist in London. It presented a likeness of Dew that bore not even the most remote resemblance to him.

It was good, then, to get from Dew himself, after his triumphant return, a true account of the ocean race and the arrest.

"You know," he began, "I once overheard a colleague at The Yard say of me, 'At least he never gets in a flap'. I tell you, though, that I was in a very genuine flap from the moment I boarded the *Laurentic*, I did not *know* if Crippen was indeed on the *Montrose*. Had I misjudged? Had I misled Sir Melville? Was I wasting valuable time sailing across the Atlantic? Was this the worst possible way to end my career? We made many, many attempts to contact the *Montrose* from the *Laurentic*'s wireless room, hour after hour after hour, but none succeeded. I lurched back and forth between quite sure and not at all sure that Crippen was on his ship. I finally heard by Marconigram on the *Laurentic* that Crippen and Le Neve had been identified as having purchased tickets for passage on the Montrose, I still could not be sure that they had boarded her.

"And although I was told that we were easily going to get ahead of the *Montrose*, I was still scared that the case was going to blow up. The newspapers had got onto my departure before I even arrived in Liverpool. I was afraid that they might somehow get in touch with the *Montrose*, and tip off Crippen. I was even more afraid that Canadian reporters would take a boat out to the *Montrose*, find Crippen and take him ashore somewhere to pump him for his story. My nightmare was that I could see them smuggling him ashore, beyond my reach, then him escaping and disappearing in the United States. A flap indeed, or at least some shaky nerves and tension, hour after hour."

Dew told us how aggressive the Canadian and American reporters had been while, on shore in Quebec, he awaited the arrival of the *Montrose*.

"They offered me bribes to arrange for them to take photographs of Crippen, and of Le Neve in her boy's suit; I refused. They waylaid me in my quarters, at meals, and on the street; I refused to be interviewed. Back home, it was reported that my own wife thought Mrs. Crippen was still alive; absolute fiction, of course.

"The press-men got even more aggressive as the *Montrose* approached. All of them had purchased tickets to travel on the *Montrose* as soon as they could get aboard. We heard that one group of reporters even planned to get out on the river on a raft, and pretend to be in distress so that the *Montrose* would pick them up before any other reporters could get to her.

"The Canadian police and I had to use every tactic from polite persuasion to threats of arrest to get them under some control. In the end, they agreed not to hinder me, and I promised to give them three long blasts on the *Montrose's* horn if Crippen and Le Neve were indeed on board. They could then come aboard, with their tickets, but I would by then have Crippen and Le Neve locked up and out of reach."

Dew nodded at Holmes, with a smile.

"Holmes, you had suggested that I might be able to board the *Montrose* from the pilot boat. A smart idea, that; and thank you. The Dominion police not only liked the idea, they even borrowed a pilot's uniform of roughly my size, so that I would not look out of place. Captain Kendall approved. The Canadian police with me posed as customs officers. And so there I was at last, on the pilot boat, approaching the *Montrose* off Father Point in the Gulf of St. Lawrence, and still not dead sure that I was going to find Crippen. Right behind us was a whole fleet of boats engaged by the press-men.

"I and the Canadian officers went first to the bridge on the *Montrose*, to meet Captain Kendall. To my relief, he told me that he was more sure than ever that he indeed had Crippen and Le Neve on board.

"He had been told in Antwerp that Crippen and Le Neve, in her boy's suit, were father and son, from Detroit in America – Mister John Philo Robinson and Master John George Robinson. It did not take him long to see through that.

"He said that they were altogether too chummy and lovey-dovey to be father and son. He almost instantly concluded that the son was in fact a girl. She looked and spoke and walked and moved like a girl, and Crippen treated her like one, holding her hand when he thought nobody was looking, and all that nonsense.

"Captain Kendall had intelligently confiscated all the newspapers on board so that Crippen and Le Neve would not see anything about themselves. Then he took one of those newspapers with a photograph of Crippen in it, and used some chalk to hide Crippen's big moustache. A smart man, Kendall. So he thus had a photo of a clean-shaven Crippen in front of him. He did much the same with a newspaper photograph of Miss Le Neve, using cut-out cardboard to isolate and focus on her face. He found she had a striking resemblance to Master Robinson."

And so the game was up, Kendall now was certain that he indeed had Crippen and Miss Le Neve on board. Dew told us how Kendall swore his officers to secrecy, and they treated Crippen in exactly the same professional and polite way as all their other passengers. The crew gave nothing away.

"Captain Kendall's problem was that he was well out of wireless range of anyone and anything. Should he carry on to Canada or steam to England? He decided to continue on course, and said he was most relieved when he approached Quebec and regained wireless contact with his owners' agent and then with me on the *Laurentic*."

I could not wait to ask the first of many questions. 'When did you first spot Crippen?'

"From Captain Kendall's bridge. Looking down on Crippen, who was on the deck below, I could not be absolutely sure it was him, but he was the right height – five foot three or four – and the right build. His hair looked right, too, brown and sandy, and bald on top.

"I had him summoned to the captain's cabin. For half a second, I almost did not recognise him, he having no more moustache and no glasses.

"But then I looked directly into his eyes – those distinctive eyes – and I knew him. It took a second for him to recognise me, in my pilot's uniform, but then he did. He gasped, and his Adam's apple began to twitch in his throat.

"We locked him in a cabin, with a Dominion police officer with him as a guard. Then we went after Le Neve.

"She recognised me instantly as I entered her cabin, and almost fainted. I had to help her to stay upright. She was wearing her brown boy's suit, by the way. As with Crippen, I placed her under arrest and locked her in a cabin with a police guard and a stewardess from the *Montrose*.

"Then I had Captain Kendall give the press-men their three long blasts on the ship's horn. The army of reporters scrambled aboard, and tried every trick in the journalistic handbook, but none got to Crippen, Le Neve, or to us policemen. And the captain's crew obeyed his orders and kept their mouths shut. The reporters had to rely on accounts from passengers."

Holmes broke in, actually clapping his hands enthusiastically. "Well done, Dew, very well done. What a gamble you and Sir Melville took on steaming off to Canada like that, but you were right, and you won. Well played indeed."

"Lucky it worked out. I heard that Superintendent Froest was less than happy when he found out Sir Melville had authorised me to go. Frosty was sure I was indeed on a useless chase. The good news is that my boss, Chief Constable Bigham of the C. I. D., and the big boss, the Commissioner, Sir Edward Henry, both approved."

Dew shrugged, and continued his story. "We searched Crippen and found he had used safety pins to make a sort of pocket in his under-vest, and had concealed some jewellery there; I recognised items that he had told me, at Hilldrop Crescent, belonged to his wife.

"We also found on him two notes, written in his hand. Taken together, they suggested that he was planning to kill himself, or, in the alternative, that he was planning, perhaps, to disappear, and to leave behind a misleading note to suggest he had committed suicide. I told him he had better not try anything on with us. He said he would not, and he did not.

"When we docked, there were several hundred curious people awaiting us on shore, even at ten o'clock at night. It took a strong escort of Canadian police to help me get Crippen and Le Neve ashore; and take him to the local gaol and her to the home of a police officer and his family. It was worse when we got them to court the next morning; there was a huge mob – there must have been well over two thousand people outside and trying to get in. Most of them did not, of course. So we pulled it off, got Crippen into court, and Crippen said he would not challenge his arrest in Canada or his removal to England.

"The press had questioned every passenger on the ship, and most of the crew. The crew gave them nothing, but passengers gave them endless tidbits about Crippen and Miss Le Neve; what they had done and said and the meals they had eaten, and so on.

"Not content with all this, the reporters continued to make up stories wholesale. They said Crippen had confessed; he absolutely had not; believe me. He never came close to admitting anything. The first thing he said to me on the *Montrose* was, 'I am not sorry. The anxiety has been too much.'

"And then he said, 'It is only fair to say that she knows nothing about it. I never told her anything.' But we never could get him to tell us just what *it* was.

"The reporters said we had confirmed that the remains at Hilldrop Crescent were female; we had not. They said Crippen had been in possession of a revolver on the Montrose; he had not. They said I arrested Crippen in front of all the passengers; I did not. They said Le Neve tried to commit suicide by swallowing a lethal pill; she did not.

"They pursued and harassed us for interviews. They offered money. They offered a lot of money, and then even more money; in the end, as the bidding rose, hundreds and hundreds of pounds. They woke me up in the middle of the night. They tried everything, but I said never a word, and they never, ever, got anywhere near Crippen or Le Neve.

"It took much effort to maintain my poise, to remain silent, and to wait for the Canadian authorities to do their part under the law, and to make arrangements to get Crippen and his mistress on a ship back to England. Mitchell was sent to assist me and to bring legal papers for the Dominion authorities. He also brought two wardresses from Holloway Prison – I had suggested a matron – to accompany Le Neve. Crippen and Le Neve remained in custody, of course.

"We arranged, under false names, to sail from Quebec, on the *Megantic,* a sister ship of the *Laurentic.* She was to leave for Liverpool on Saturday August 20th.

"We took carriages to a country wharf in Quebec, and had a small steamer awaiting us there. And off we set to meet with the *Megantic* as she steamed down the river. The arrangements had all been made in secrecy, but a crafty press-man had engaged his own steamer, and almost caught up to us. He did not quite make it, though, and had to settle for a picture of our party boarding the *Megantic,* from some distance away."

"And so, on August 20th, we sailed for home on the *Megantic.* We found that one persistent and crafty press fellow from England had contrived to be aboard, with a legitimate ticket, but we managed to keep him away from Crippen and Le Neve, and, of course, we kept them away from each other."

I had more questions that I threw at Dew. "How did the journey go? How was Crippen? How did he take his arrest? What did he say? Did he admit anything?"

"Admit? He said not a word about the case, Dr. Watson, not a word. I mean it; not a word. Mitchell and I talked often with him but no matter how craftily we placed our questions, Crippen just smiled, ignored the question, and carried on the conversation. It was much the same with Miss Le Neve; she and I talked quite often, but the case was entirely out of bounds. She was pleasant enough, but, honestly, she is not the brightest candle in the cathedral. I have no idea what she and Crippen see in each other."

I directed a question to him. "Do you think she is guilty?"

"Of being involved in the murder? No, I think not. At first, she appeared to be stunned and in shock. She said nothing, literally nothing. When I told her about our discovery of the remains, she kept insisting, 'Oh, no, no, Mrs. Crippen went to America and she died there of an illness'. That was the most I could get out of her. She desperately wanted to get out of the boy's suit and into women's clothing. I helped her purchase some. She was most grateful – but still never said a word about the case.

"All in all, I think she knew nothing about the murder or the remains. Still, as a police officer I have to leave the door open, and we continue to look for evidence of her *rôle*. Right now, she is still charged with murder and mutilation, although accessory after the fact might fit better. Over to the Crown lawyers on that."

Holmes topped up Dew's glass, and the chief inspector continued his account.

"On the *Megantic*, Crippen talked about his early life in America. He talked about the political news. He talked about London, and he talked about France. He talked about food. He talked about the voyage and the weather. He talked about the theatre – but never about the music-hall world. Not one word about his wife and Hilldrop Crescent could we get out of him. He talked about books, and he read a basketful during the voyage. He loves crime novels. We did not allow him to have any of those on the voyage, but we did bring him books of our choosing from the ship's library.

"Crippen was no trouble at all, at any time. He did not at all seem or act like a man accused of murder heading home for trial and probably the gallows. He was talkative and friendly – it was hard not to like him, if you please – and he asked constantly after Miss Le Neve and her welfare.

"I did not permit them to get together or exchange messages. But as we approached Liverpool on the 27th, Crippen asked if he might be permitted to see her, if from some distance. He promised he would not attempt to speak to her. I said I would permit this if Miss Le Neve wished it, and she did. So I let them stand, well guarded, in the doorways of their separate cabins, about 30 feet apart, and see each other. I had told them firmly not to say anything to each other, and they obeyed. Neither said a word, but they exchanged a little wave.

"Then we steamed into Liverpool. I knew that there could be scores of reporters and a big crowd awaiting us. Chief Inspector Duckworth of the Liverpool police came out in a tug, early on in our approach. We had thought of taking our prisoners off by boat, of course, but the wind blew up a bit and the water became quite choppy. We could not see Miss Le Neve and the wardresses clambering down a ship's ladder to Duckworth's tug in those conditions.

"What we did, when we docked, was to bring the prisoners, separately, down the crew's gangway at the stern, rather than by the main passengers' gangway in the centre of the ship. We had Crippen all bundled up in my Ulster coat and hat so that you could not really see his face.

"But, do you know, that did not fool one young man in the crowd. He rushed at Crippen and was waving a cane. We fended him off, with the help of some soldiers who had been on the *Megantic*, slipped into the customs shed by a side-door, then made a dash, between lines of policemen, for the London boat train. While the reporters were madly looking for me and Crippen, the two wardresses from Holloway, Miss Stone and Miss Foster, quietly brought Miss Le Neve ashore, and they, too, managed to evade the press people. And so we got to the boat train to London without a mishap.

"If there was a big crowd in Liverpool, there was a far greater one on our arrival at Euston, scores upon scores of them, all booing and jeering Crippen and Le Neve. But there were more than a hundred police officers on duty, keeping the crowd back, and they had cordoned off part of Platform 1 with barriers. So we got the two away successfully, and off to Bow Street.

"There was a huge crowd there, too, outside the police station, all shouting at Crippen and threatening to string him up then and there. One section of the crowd did attempt to rush us, but our lads at Bow Street managed to close the gates on the mob as we entered, and so we were safe.

"Mitchell and I were very glad to hand over our prisoners, sign all the paperwork, and bring our travels to a successful end."

Holmes began again to clap, and I joined him with equal enthusiasm. Dew raised his glass. "Thank you, gentlemen. But I am sure we could not have done so well – and perhaps not at all – without your own assistance. Credit where credit is due!"

Dew obtained for me a prized seat in the crowded courtroom when Crippen and Le Neve appeared in the Bow Street magistrate's court.

It was, of course, the first time I had seen Crippen in person, a short, balding man with slightly protruberant eyes and a sandy moustache that was but partly grown back after being removed during his flight. He looked tired. Miss Le Neve was dressed in blue, and her face was hidden by a blue veil beneath a big blue hat. The pair was quickly remanded in custody for eight days.

Chapter Nine

Holmes continued to work impossibly long, long hours with Dew and Mitchell now that they were home.

With them, I was permitted to attend a meeting of the doctors in the case. It was on Friday September 2nd, four days before the presentation of the Crown's evidence to the magistrate's court, that Drs. Spilsbury, Willcox and Pepper, and Chief Inspector Dew, joined us for dinner at 221B, Baker Street. The thought of returning to Sussex (where a neighbouring farmer was keeping an experienced eye on Holmes's precious bees) had long been gone from my friend's mind.

The conversation at our table instantly turned to Crippen, of course, and Dew assured our guests that he and they could trust us to keep confidential anything spoken of there.

There followed much important discussion about the piece of skin recovered from the shallow grave at Hilldrop Crescent. I gathered that it measured some six inches in width, and seven in length, and our doctors were sure that it carried a significant scar. I made the following notes:

Pepper:- 'Marshall and I examined the specimen carefully on Monday August 8th. There is no doubt in my mind that it was an old scar, although whether from a wound or from a surgical operation I could not determine. There were hairs on the skin that I am fully satisfied are pubic hairs, so that helped to locate the piece of skin and the scar. The scar looked exactly like those I have seen before as the result of an operation on the lower abdomen.'

Marshall:- 'I examined the specimen with Pepper on August 8th. I, too, am quite sure that it is a scar. I was aware, by way of Chief Inspector Dew, that Cora Crippen had undergone an operation in the past but I assure you that this information in no way influenced my judgement. A scar it was and a scar it is.'

Willcox:- 'I concur. I too examined it on August 8th, and it is certainly a scar, on a piece of skin from the lower wall of the abdomen.'

(A few days later, Bernard Spilsbury examined the specimen himself and added his own view. 'I am quite satisfied that it was the scar from an old operation. There is no room for doubt about this. I agree that the hairs thereon are pubic hairs.')

On top of this, of course, was other physical evidence: the dyed hair similar to that of Mrs. Crippen, the hair curler of a type she used (in fact, two more such Hinde's curlers had been found among the remains) and the camisole identified as similar to those owned and worn by Mrs. Crippen.

Add to these the fact that no *other* woman with such a scar and dyed or bleached hair had been reported missing, and the odds, then, were that the remains dug up at 39 ,Hilldrop Crescent indeed were those of Cora Crippen. Holmes and the others were fully satisfied that we had confirmation of the victim's identity.

Then Dr. Willcox set off his giant bombshell.

"You have been awaiting, gentlemen, the results of my toxicological tests. I have completed them, and am prepared to testify on oath that Mrs. Crippen was killed by a large overdose of hyoscine hydrobromide."

There was a collective shout of surprise and applause, and Dew pounded the table with his right fist so hard that the plates and cutlery and glasses rattled and danced. "Got him, got him, got him! The hyoscine that he purchased back in January."

All eyes and ears turned to Willcox.

"The tests are a little complex, and certainly time-consuming, but I am absolutely positive in their outcome. In my estimation, the dose administered was massive. After all this time, and with only partial remains to examine, I found there to be almost one-third of a grain present. As you doctors know, the normal sedative dose would be one one-hundredth of a grain, or perhaps two one-hundredths in a stubborn case. A quarter-grain could be fatal; a third or a half-grain would most certainly be so."

Dew thumped the table again, and repeated this action when Willcox made his next point.

"You know, we must thank our lucky stars for the quicklime that was used in an attempt to destroy the remains. Instead, it helped preserve the organs, and without that I might never have found the hyoscine."

Now Holmes broke in. "Sergeant Crutchett and I have unearthed a witness who is ready to testify that Crippen had purchased two sacks of lime from him. However, Travers Humphreys, speaking for the Director of Public Prosecutions, finds the man to be potentially weak on the positive identification of Crippen, so it may be that the Crown will not call him."

Holmes now addressed Dr. Willcox. "How might the hyoscine have been administered? And what would have then happened?"

"Administered by mouth, certainly. But hydrobromide of hyoscine is just a little bitter, so I would guess that he would serve it to her in some food or drink to disguise that. We found no traces of food, therefore in a drink, I would suggest. As for the immediate effects, Holmes, she would very quickly lose consciousness. Paralysis would set in, and, I would say, she would be dead within an hour. I have so advised the Crown."

I now broke in. "Poison in a large and pretty fast-acting dose. So much the supposed screeches, screams and gunshots. Has anybody yet found any remaining hyoscine anywhere? The remains of what he purchased in January? Or did he give her the lot?"

"To the first question, no, although we have looked carefully." That came from Holmes.

"To the second question, to say so definitively would be speculative, but from my findings I think it highly probable." That was from Dr. Willcox.

The doctors went on to debate the evidence that each had discussed with the Crown, and would be called to deliver in court. Chief Inspector Dew obliged us with a summary of the detailed case that he and other Crown witnesses could be expected to deliver.

"Mind you, I expect that snake Newton will arrange for Crippen's team of barristers to give us as good a bullying as witnesses ever are subjected to."

"Arch-snake," said Holmes, and gave me an explanation. "Arthur Newton is Crippen's solicitor in this case. Newton is a schemer, a trickster and without scruples. How he became engaged by Crippen is not known to us. If there is a loophole in a case, though, Newton will find it, but I fully expect that one day he will end up in the dock himself."

"He already has," said Dew. "Did you not know? Twenty years ago. He tried to persuade three young men not to testify in a gross indecency case involving a male house of ill repute in Cleveland Street. Newton was sentenced to six weeks for conspiracy to pervert justice. How he was not then struck off as a lawyer I shall never know. I do know that if Crippen has any money, Newton will have the lot, and will steal the socks and shoes off Crippen's feet while he is at it."

On Tuesday September 6th, we attended the Bow Street magistrate's court, where Drs. Pepper and Willcox gave their dramatic evidence. Crippen appeared stunned as Willcox revealed the presence of the hydrobromide of hyoscine in the remains. Crippen's face quickly turned a shocking red, then white. He said nothing. The case was once more adjourned, however, and once again, before and after the hearing, angry crowds in the street shouted foul epithets at the accused.

On September 21st, we were back at Bow Street again, to hear the presiding magistrate, Sir Albert de Rutzen, declare that there was sufficient evidence to warrant sending Crippen and Le Neve for trial at the Old Bailey. Newton declared that both would plead not guilty. He went on, we learnt, to collect some of his legal fees by way of an auction of Crippen's effects at 39, Hilldrop Crescent. It came to light later that Newton had also sought to sell Crippen's life story to an American newspaper. A shady trickster, indeed.

We were ready now for the inquest to conclude, and the trial to begin. The inquest ended on the 26th, with the jury returning a verdict of death by murder.

On October 11th, the remains of Cora Crippen were buried in the Roman Catholic cemetery of St. Pancras in East Finchley. This was authorised by a coroner's order of September 26th. The ceremony was well attended by members of the Music Hall Ladies' Guild.

Crippen's trial in the Central Criminal Court at the Old Bailey was set to begin a week later, on Tuesday October 18th. (The Crown had by now decided to try Le Neve separately, and later, on the lesser charge of being an accessory after the fact.) On Saturday the 15th, Holmes and I were permitted to attend a meeting at which the Crown for the Crippen trial was represented by Richard Muir, Travers Humphreys and Samuel Ingleby Oddie.

The handsome Muir was a man to whom, it seemed, work was life. He would regularly be first in his office each day, and the last to leave. And while colleagues may have taken weekends off, Muir was never known to have so done. He never missed a trick in court, either, but Holmes made a private comment:- 'He is so meticulous in presenting endless detail that he sometimes loses touch with the audience'.

In what amounted to a final dress rehearsal on that Saturday, Muir led us (meticulously indeed) through his proposed opening remarks, his list of witnesses and what each would say, the perceived strengths and weaknesses of the Crown's case, and what to expect from Crippen's barrister,

Alfred Tobin; a man not as well known as Muir but, as Muir put it, 'no fool at all'.

"My simple thesis, gentlemen, is this: Crippen had been hard up for money. His affections were fixed upon his mistress. Upon his wife's death, their money and property would be all Crippen's, and now he would be able to keep and support Le Neve."

His deputy, Travers Humphreys, interjected. "Tobin could argue that we have little evidence of a pecuniary motive. Crippen had some income, he had money in the bank. What did he gain from his wife's death? A couple of hundred from pawning her jewellery that he says was really his, anyway?"

Muir shrugged, with a friendly smile. "The question is not what you or I or Tobin accept, Humphreys. It is what the jury will accept."

Humphreys persisted:- "Another thesis is that it is more likely that Miss Le Neve was pressuring him for marriage."

Muir shrugged again. "We have no evidence that she was doing that, no matter how likely it was."

During a pause in the conversation, I dared to weigh in with a question myself. "Thinking of motive, could it be possible that Mrs. Crippen had become aware of her husband's affair with Miss Le Neve? That she threatened to expose Crippen, and he killed her as a result. I have been wondering about it since we learnt that Mrs. Crippen had tried, unsuccessfully, to withdraw their six hundred pounds from the bank. Was she planning to leave Crippen and disappear with all his money? If so, was it because she had found out about Crippen and Le Neve?"

Muir responded. "Good, Dr. Watson, good. Fair questions, those. We know that Mrs. Crippen was aware of Ethel Le Neve's role in his offices. We also know that Mrs. Crippen went to his offices occasionally, and saw Le Neve there. Crippen himself says he is sure that Mrs. Crippen did not know of his affair with Miss Le Neve. Miss Le Neve says Mrs. Crippen 'treated me as a friend', but William Long, Crippen's employee, says Mrs. Crippen treated her simply and normally as one of her husband's employee. As for the affair, we have no reliable evidence that Mrs. Crippen knew or suspected it, I regret."

Muir led us at length through his list of witnesses, and after each invited the lawyers present to give their opinions.

"We shall start with Frederick Lown, the owner of 39, Hilldrop Crescent. He will will testify that he let the house to Crippen on 21st September 1905 and that on 16th March this year Crippen told him that he was giving three months notice of ending the rental and that Mrs. Crippen had gone to America. Mr. Lown saw Crippen again in June of this year, and Crippen told him that his wife had died in America.

"Dr. John Herbert Burroughs, a friend of the Crippens, will testify as to how, in response to a letter of condolence that he and his wife sent to Crippen, Crippen responded on black-edged mourning paper. He will also describe how the Crippens seemed to get along well, although Mrs. Crippen could be sometimes hasty in he manner in which she treated her husband.

"Clara Martinetti will testify about having dinner at the Crippen home on January 31st, and how she never saw Belle Elmore alive after that. She will describe at length what Crippen subsequently said about his wife's so-called disappearance and supposed death in America. She will also testify about Mrs. Crippen's scar.

"Louise Smythson of the Music Hall Ladies' Guild will talk about the presence of Miss Le Neve at the ball of the Music Hall Benevolent Fund, wearing Mrs. Crippen's jewellery. Mrs. Smythson will also testify about the stories that Crippen told about his wife's alleged death.

"I will call Teresa Hunn, Mrs. Crippen's American sister. She, too, will testify about Mrs. Crippen's surgery and scar.

"Then we will have the other American witness, Mr. Bruce Miller. He will insist that his relationship with Mrs. Crippen was affectionate but not intimate. The jury can decide for themselves whether to believe him.

"Miss Melinda May of the Music Hall Ladies' Guild will testify about Crippen's stories and lies, and will also identify pieces of Mrs. Crippen's jewellery, and testify as to her bleached hair.

"Mrs. Emily Jackson, Le Neve's landlady, will tell the court what she knows of Miss Le Neve's relationship with Crippen."

Muir kept referring to his notes as he talked. I could see from where I sat that they were long and carefully organised, with various words and sections underlined in inks of different colours. As he went on and on, I could see why Holmes had spoken of Muir's penchant for endless detail, to the point where he sometimes lost his audience.

Still, it was interesting to hear his team of lawyers weighing in with many challenging questions and comments. So did Dew, Mitchell, and Holmes. Indeed, it was Holmes who led to the hammering home of the final nail.

"Anything overlooked?" was a question that Muir asked as we reached the end of his agenda.

Holmes then raised the question of the pyjama jacket that we found in the grave at 39, Hilldrop Crescent.

Dew had discovered on July 14th, in a box under a bed at Hilldrop Crescent, two complete pyjama suits, and a pair of striped pyjama trousers without their jacket. Those lone trousers certainly looked like a perfect match to the striped pyjama jacket found with the body in the coal-cellar grave. The name of the maker, Jones Brothers of Holloway, was on this jacket. What had Jones Brothers of Holloway to tell us about this? Could they link the jacket to Crippen. Is there any evidence that he purchased it? If so, when?

Sergeant Mitchell chided Holmes. "Ah, we did not forget that, Mr. Holmes, sir, not likely. One of our men went to Jones Brothers, but he had no luck. The clerk there was sure of nothing. He said he could not help. They may sell pyjamas but it seems that they do not keep records of who purchases them."

Holmes retorted sharply. "Oh, not so. I have myself purchased pyjamas from them, and my newest dressing gown, no less. They recorded those sales in detail in their ledger, and gave to me full receipts. Your man may have misunderstood, or the clerk was being less than helpful. I know the manager there. I will pursue him, if you wish."

Mitchell lit up with anger. "It was one of my lads that went to Jones Brothers to investigate. I will have his bowels for braces if he has let us down. I will get another constable to go there and try again."

With his usual impatience and insistence upon doing almost everything himself, my friend went without his luncheon and, dragging a still-steaming Sergeant Mitchell with him, headed for Jones Brothers' Holloway establishment with a list of questions from Muir.

Thus it was that the Crown and the New Scotland Yard teams determined at the last minute that pyjamas made from the striped material in question were available from Jones Brothers only after late December 1908 and that (imagine here a fanfare of trumpets and a crash of cymbals) pyjamas of that material were delivered to 39, Hilldrop Crescent on January 5th, 1909, cash on delivery.

A relieved Mitchell gave Holmes a clumsy pat on the back, and gave the police team's conclusion:- "Crippen's goose is cooked. If that jacket was not made until December 1908, it could not have got in with the remains until well *after* Crippen had moved into Hilldrop Crescent in 1905. Add that to Dr. Pepper's opinion on how long the body had been buried, and Crippen is done for."

"Not so fast," said Muir, as the discussion resumed after luncheon. "Do we not have to let the defence know about this pyjama business? It amounts to new evidence found at the very last minute. Must we not advise the defence?"

Travers Humphreys protested, warmly. "That would certainly mean an adjournment. Can we not finesse it? We are told that Crippen is going to testify in his own defence. We could ask him about the suits of pyjamas and when he bought them. Then could we not call Mr. Holmes's fellow from Jones Brothers, and get the dates – and his testimony about the material – into the record?"

The lawyers argued back and forth and, if I understood them correctly, decided to go ahead without advising the defence that they could link Crippen to the pyjama jacket found with the body.

Muir turned to Detective Sergeant Mitchell. "Chief Inspector Dew tells me that you have reservations about Adelene Harrison as a Crown witness, although we have her on our list."

"Yes, sir. To be honest, I think she could be difficult. She simply cannot answer a question in a few words, and launches into long answers that quickly turn into long speeches. She barely stops for breath. I think she might have an unfortunate impact on the jury. However, she does know everything there is to know about Mrs. Crippen's clothes and jewellery, Mrs. Crippen's hair and her bleaching her hair, and even knows about Mrs. Crippen's undergarments. So Mrs. Harrison might help with the question of identification of the remains, sir, if you can hold her answers down to 'yes' and 'no', and no speech-making."

"Thank you. That is roughly what Mr. Dew told me, and I accept your advice. She can help with identification, and that is positive. I shall try to keep her from detours and diversions. You mention her knowledge of Mrs. Crippen's jewellery. We have another witness who, I think, would be hard to match in that regard. That is the Miss Melinda May, the secretary of the Music Hall Ladies' Guild. As you know, I will be asking her to identify the jewellery we will enter."

Muir turned to the group, and asked once more:- "Now, anything overlooked?"

This time, there was a collective shaking of heads, and nobody spoke.

"There we are, then," concluded Muir. "Let us see if we can find some worthwhile employment for Mr. Ellis."

Again, I was a layman lost, but Holmes addressed me with a grim smile.

"John Ellis is a barber and news-agent from Rochdale. He is also one of our official hangmen."

Chapter Ten

A milling, babbling crowd of hundreds jammed the street outside the Central Criminal Court, the Old Bailey, built upon the land where the infamous Newgate Prison had once stood.

Comparatively few managed to get in to the Number 1 courtroom, however, as the court had, for this trial, established a system of half-day public admission tickets. Several thousand people had applied for them. Dew, though, had arranged for Holmes and me to have the red and blue tickets necessary for both to attend the full trial, and he had somehow managed to arrange good seats for us, with 'Reserved for Official Court Use' signs prominently attached to them.

And so, on Tuesday October 18th, 1910, the trial of the century began before the Lord Chief Justice, the Right Honourable Lord Alverstone, better known to Holmes from earlier in his legal career as Dickie Webster. To begin, the clerk of the court intoned solemnly the question:-

"Hawley Harvey Crippen, you are indicted and also charged on the coroner's inquisition with the wilful murder of Cora Crippen on the 1st February last. Are you guilty or not guilty?"

"Not guilty, my lord."

And so Prosecutor Muir and his team prepared to battle with the lead barrister for the defence, Alfred Tobin, and his men. (Holmes had informed me as we entered the court:-

"Tobin is not bad as a lawyer, but a work-horse rather than a race-horse. I hear that they really wanted Edward Marshall Hall but could not reach agreement with him and so he returned the brief.")

Muir told the court and jury in his opening statement that Crippen had been hard up for money, and that his affections had been fixed upon Miss Le Neve. As the official court reporter captured it:-

"For three years, he had immoral relations with her of a clandestine kind, never staying away from home at night, but meeting her in hotels in the daytime."

Mr. Muir continued:- "If Belle Elmore died ... Belle Elmore's money, and property which could be converted into money, would enable him to keep Ethel Le Neve, which at that time he was unable to do."

He drove home in his address how Crippen knew his wife would never appear again.

"He at once began to convert her property, and on 12th March Ethel Le Neve, who had been seen wearing a brooch and furs belonging to Belle Elmore, went permanently to live with him at 39, Hilldrop Crescent. Crippen was therefore quite certain that his wife would never return, but he did not tell her friends he knew that she would never return. He started a campaign of lies to account for her disappearance.

"He knew that if his wife did not attend the meeting of the Music Hall Ladies' Guild on 2nd February inquiries would be made, and so he sent by the hand of Le Neve two letters to the Guild and to Miss May, one of the officials of the Guild. Then came the story of her disappearance to America, and the invention of further lies, because a visit to America might be expected to terminate at some time or other, to account for the fact that she was never to return.

"On 23rd March he told Mrs. Martinetti that he had very bad news, and was momentarily expecting worse. He said that if anything should happen to Belle he was going to France for a week.

"Mrs. Martinetti said, 'Whatever for?'

"He said, 'Oh, I shall want a change.'

"The truth being that at that time he had arranged an Easter trip to Dieppe with Ethel Le Neve. The slate had to be wiped clean of Belle Elmore before he started, and from Victoria on the early morning of 24th March he sent the telegram to Mrs. Martinetti stating that Belle died the previous night at six o'clock.

"And that nothing should remain to interfere with the rest he was seeking in France, he sent the advertisement to *The Era* announcing that Belle Elmore had died in California – no nearer than that – on 23rd March The object of the advertisement was to stop people asking a lot of questions.

"But Belle Elmore's friends were not prevented from asking a lot of questions, and they got some answers .... It must have been obvious to Crippen then that his statements with regard to the disappearance of Belle Elmore were being doubted, and it was perfectly plain after his interview with Chief Inspector Dew that it was useless to proceed with the stories he had told."

"Then Crippen fled, although," said Muir, "he had nothing to fly from – not if his statement was true, that as far as he knew, Belle Elmore was alive.

"But he fled. What he fled from was found on 13th July, when under the brick floor in the cellar of the house in Hilldrop Crescent where Belle Elmore was last seen alive on 1st February, where she was left alone at half-past one in the morning of that day with the prisoner, the police found human remains ....

"Whose could those human remains be but the remains of Belle Elmore, and who but Crippen could have put them there?"

Tobin, for the defence, argued in his opening speech that the Crown had not identified the remains.

"Never mind what their suspicions might be; they must prove beyond all doubt that those remains were the remains of a woman, and those of Belle Elmore, or else the prisoner was entitled as a right to be acquitted.

"The first outstanding feature in the evidence was Dr. Crippen's reputation amongst those who knew him best and had known him for long years. From every witness who had known him came the same tale; these were the characteristics in the very words the witnesses had used 'amiable', 'kind-hearted', 'good-hearted', 'good-tempered', 'one of the nicest men I ever met'.

"The people who gave him that character were people of different ages, of different interests, and of both sexes. Could the jury say that that reputation was not deservedly earned? Yet it was openly suggested that a man with those characteristics suddenly became a fiend incarnate."

Tobin went on to dismiss the Crown's theory that Crippen murdered his wife for money. "Crippen was not in debt, and he could not draw a single farthing from the deposit account in the Charing Cross Bank until after twelve months' notice."

You can see in the official records of the trial that Tobin asked if it could really be said that Crippen murdered his wife in February in order to marry his mistress?

"He did not fly from the country with his mistress until the month of July. He had never married her, and surely that could not be a motive.

"It was suggested that this man criminally abused the skill and dexterity of a surgeon and a man well versed in anatomy, and removed all trace of sex, the head, the hands, the feet, and the bones. Had he that dexterity? He did not practise in anatomy; he had never conducted a *post-mortem* in his life; he knew nothing of anatomy or operations except what he had learned in his student days, long years ago.

"His manner at the time of the alleged murder, and for months afterwards, could not be wiped aside. Just before the wife's disappearance, and for months afterwards, he showed no sign of agitation, no sign of fright, no seeking to avoid his friends and his wife's friends.

"Dr. Crippen showed no signs of constraint at the dinner party on 31st January, and yet it was suggested that he was shortly to give the poison he had bought some twelve days before to the woman who was sitting at the other end of the table. The next day he went to work as usual, having, it was suggested by the Crown, murdered his wife and left her body in the house alone. He could not have got rid of the bones, the head, the hands, and the feet, and buried the flesh in the few short hours between 1:30 a.m. and his going to his work next morning.

"At the very time that he was going about his business, and calling on his friends as usual, showing no sign of terror, if he was the murderer, he was cutting up the body in his house, and carrying away the remains piecemeal. It was said that he had the night-time to do these things in. Was it conceivable that he could have done that without somebody noticing something? Could he have spent the long hours through the night at home after his work doing things like that, without any trace being visible on his face when he went to his work at the usual hours day by day?

"It was suggested that he took Le Neve to live over the remains of the wife he had murdered. Did they believe that, if he had murdered his wife, and recently buried her remains in his cellar, he would have left his house for those days when he took Le Neve to Dieppe? There was no proof whatever that he had ever had a surgical knife; there was no trace of blood found anywhere in the house; as regards the suggestion that he buried the remains, no pickaxe to get out the bricks had been traced; and there was no proof of the purchase of any lime by him."

Tobin told the jury-men that Crippen would go into the witness-box and tell his side of the story. He would be followed by doctors who would counter the Crown's medical evidence, and 'an expert in poisons of high reputation' who would testify that an alkaloid found in the remains might not have been a vegetable alkaloid introduced into the body during life, but an animal alkaloid produced by the ordinary process of putrefaction in a dead body.

We had been advised of this, of course, and I much looked forward to hearing an opposing scientific analysis of the poison, and of whether the 'scar' was or was not a scar.

The court reporter's notes show how Tobin asked the jury to forget all the newspaper coverage of the case.

"Every man and woman in the land had discussed this case, and the danger of it was that they only partially knew the facts. All that publicity to gratify the public taste must be fraught with a grave danger to the administration of justice, because it was human nature that the man who read these columns should inevitably take a view regarding Dr. Crippen before his trial. They knew how difficult it was to wipe the slate clean, and to approach the case with an absolutely open mind. He knew, however, that the jury were determined, so far as their will power would enable them, to do their best to try."

And so the trial began.

The early witnesses that Muir called included two Americans, Theresa Hunn, known as Tessie, who was Belle Elmore's younger sister, and Bruce Miller, the former one-man band, identified as a lover of Mrs. Crippen.

Mrs. Hunn testified that she saw a fresh scar on Belle Elmore's stomach in 1893 or thereabouts. "It was not all healed, it was fresh. I saw that scar again seven years ago; it was healed much better then than it was first time I saw it. It would be about 4 or 5 inches long and about one inch wide, but I could not quite exactly say. It was more a cream colour than the rest of her skin, and paler looking."

She went on to testify about a letter from Crippen – on black-edged mourning paper – that had been received by a half-sister, Mrs. Robert Mills:-

My Dear Louise and Robert,

I hardly know how to write to you of my dreadful loss. The shock to me has been so dreadful that I am hardly able to control myself. My poor Cora is gone, and, to make the shock to me more dreadful, I did not even see her at the last. A few weeks ago we had news that an old relative of mine in

California was dying, and, to secure important property for ourselves, it was necessary one of us to go and put the matter into a lawyer's hands at once. As I was very busy, Cora proposed she should go, and as it was necessary for some one to be there at once, she would go straight through from here to California without stopping at all and then return by way of Brooklyn, and she would be able to pay all of you a long visit. Unfortunately, on the way my poor Cora caught a severe cold, and not having while travelling taken proper care of herself, it has settled on her lungs, later to develop into pleuro-pneumonia. She wished not to frighten me, so kept writing not to worry about her and it was only a slight matter, and the next I heard by cable was that she was dangerously ill, and two days later after I cabled to know should I go to her I had the dreadful news that she had passed away.

Imagine if you can the dreadful shock to me never more to see my Cora alive nor hear her voice again. She is being sent back to me, and I shall soon have what is left of her here. Of course, I am giving up the house; in fact, it drives me mad to be in it alone, and I will sell out everything in a few days. I do not know what I shall do, but probably find some business to take me travelling for a few months until I can recover from the shock a little, but as soon as I have a settled address again I will write again to you.

As it is so terrible to me to have to write this dreadful news, will you please tell all the others of our loss.

Love to all. Write soon again, and give you my address probably next in France.

DOCTOR.

109

What an odd way to sign any letter, I thought. Should he not, for one thing, have signed it PATENT MEDICINE PEDLAR? Or even WIFE-MURDERER?

Then came Bruce Miller, the American one-man-band turned estate agent. He testified when questioned by Tobin that, while Crippen had been absent in America on business, he (Miller) visited Mrs. Crippen frequently.

"I would visit her two or three times a week sometimes, and then sometimes I would not see her for a week or two weeks or about three weeks. I visited her sometimes in the afternoons and sometimes in the evenings."

"Were you fond of her?"

"Yes."

"Did you ever tell her that you loved her?"

"Well, I do not know that I ever put it in that way."

"Did you indicate to her that you did love her?"

"She always understood it that way, I suppose."

"Then you did love her, I presume?"

"I do not mean to say that. I did not exactly love her; I thought a great deal of her as far as friendship was concerned. She was a married lady, and we will let it end at that. It was a platonic friendship."

"I rather gathered from the answers you gave me that you communicated to her in some way that you did love her?"

"A little present once in a while or something of that kind."

"Do you know the difference between friendship and love?"

"Yes."

"Were you more than a friend?"

" I could not be more than a friend. She was a married lady and I was a married man."

"Were you more than a friend, sir?"

"I could not be more than a friend. I was not."

At this point, the Lord Chief Justice broke in:-

"Answer the question whether you were or were not?"

"I was not more than a friend."

"Were there any improper relations between you and her?"

"No."

Tobin returned to the attack, and Miller agreed that he had written affectionate letters to Mrs. Crippen.

"Were those affectionate letters 'Love and kisses to Brown Eyes' and that kind of thing?"

"They may have been. Sometimes I wrote to her that way, and sometimes I did not."

"You are still very fond of her?"

"I should be if she were here. We have always been friends, and I should not stop now. She wrote letters back to me."

"Were her letters couched in the same kind of terms as your letters to her?"

"Perhaps not quite so endearing."

"But still they were sufficiently endearing?"

"They were friendly; they were generally very short, and they were letters that my wife has read. They did not contain endearing terms somewhat similar to those that I used when writing to her."

"Never?"

"Never."

"Did she encourage your attentions?"

"My attentions were not of the kind you are perhaps speaking of."

"I call it attentions when you write, 'Love and kisses to Brown Eyes'. Did she discourage those expressions in your letters?"

"She did not, because they were not expressed as you want to interpret them."

"Did she ever write back saying that she did not like such expressions?"

"She never did; she did not say anything about it in her letters."

He had, indeed, he admitted, given her photographs of himself as well as sending letters and presents, but, he swore again, there had been no improper relations.

Miller also testified that he not seen Mrs. Crippen since he left London for America in April 1904. Had there been any proposition of Mrs. Crippen coming to him in America?

"Never. I never heard of such a thing."

111

Miss Le Neve's former landlady, Emily Jackson, related how Le Neve had begun to sleep elsewhere in February of this year. "She stayed away one night, and then she would sleep at home, and then she would stay away two nights, and then she finally slept away from home altogether."

Also in February, Le Neve began wearing jewellery that Mrs. Jackson had not seen before. Among other items, "I saw her wear on the wedding-ring finger a plain gold band, like a gentleman's plain ring; I should not call it a wedding ring."

Then in February and March Miss Le Neve started to give Mrs. Jackson numerous items of women's clothing and jewellery, some of it brought to the Jackson house by Le Neve and Crippen himself. Mrs. Jackson was handed, and confirmed, a long list of such items.

She had kind words for Crippen:-

"Do you agree that he was a good-tempered and kind-hearted man?"

"He always gave me that impression."

"I think you said at the Police Court that you thought he was one of the nicest men you ever met?"

"I did."

Witness Frederick Pedgrift confirmed that Crippen had placed the ad in *The Era* newspaper reporting his wife's death. Then Mr. Stuart, manager of Attenboroughs, pawnbrokers, described how Crippen had pawned jewellery there on February 2nd, and again on February 9th.

Marion Curnow, manageress of Munyon's Remedies, told the court that she had known Crippen for about twelve years, and had met Mrs. Crippen.

"I first heard of her being away from London about the end of February. I asked Dr. Crippen if she was away, and he said, 'Yes, she has gone for a trip to America'. He did not give me any reason for her going.

"I first heard it said at Easter time that she was dead. I asked Dr. Crippen if he had enjoyed his holiday he had been away during the Eastertide and he said as well as he could under the circumstances. I asked him if it was true that Mrs. Crippen was dead, and he bowed his head."

Mrs. Curnow described how Crippen had given her two envelopes, at the beginning of March, that proved to contain bank deposit notes and jewellery. She knew nothing of Crippen's purchase of hyoscine; it had not been done on behalf of Munyon's. She went on to agree with Mr. Tobin's description of Crippen as 'kind-hearted and amiable'.

Tobin:- "Are you pretty confident that he came and saw you on the morning of 1ˢᵗ February?"

"I cannot remember his not coming."

"During the rest of that week, and the following fortnight, did he come regularly every day?"

"Yes."

"Did you notice any signs whatever of agitation or terror on his face?"

"No, I cannot say that I did."

"Were his manner and conversation just the same as they always had been?"

"Yes."

"No frightened or hunted look about him?"

"No."

"Nothing that you observed unusual?"

"No."

Gilbert Rylance, who had taken on Crippen as a partner in Rylance's company, The Yale Tooth Specialists, testified about a letter dated July 9ᵗʰ from Crippen, that began:-

---

Dear Dr. Rylance,

I now find that in order to escape trouble I shall be obliged to absent myself for a time.

It gave no explanation of the trouble.

Then William Long, Crippen's dental mechanic and employee, testified that Crippen was in his office unusually early on July 9ᵗʰ.

"I asked him if there was any trouble, and he said, 'Only a little scandal'. He gave no further explanation.

"He gave me a list of clothes which he sent me out to buy for him. I bought a brown tweed suit."

The Lord Chief Justice:- "Were you to buy them for a man or a woman, or what?"

"A boy .... I also bought a brown felt hat, two shirts, two collars, a tie, and a pair of boots. These were all for a boy."

Long said that after Crippen left the office, he (Long) received a letter from Crippen, asking Long to pay Crippen's rent on 39, Hilldrop Crescent, and to wind up Crippen's affairs. Long was performing this commission when the police went to the house.

Mr. Tobin:- "Take the critical time, which is early in February of this year; did he (Crippen) during that time to come daily to his work just the same as usual? Did he ever omit a single day as far as you remember?"

"No."

"Did he come at the regular times?"

"Yes."

"Did he ever show any trace of uneasiness?"

"No."

"Any worried appearance about him?"

"No."

"No hunted or worried appearance or anything of that kind; nothing unusual about his manner?"

"Nothing whatever."

"And diligent in his work as before?"

"Yes."

"No trace of abruptness as if he had got anything on his mind?"

"Not the slightest. He was just as kind as ever."

"And talking as freely and in the same way as he always did, without constraint or restraint?"

"Yes."

Edgar Brett, assistant manager of the Charing Cross Bank, now testified about Mrs. Crippen's unsuccessful attempt to withdraw six hundred pounds, in December 1909, from a joint account held by the Crippens. "With a deposit account at seven per cent, there must always be twelve months' notice of withdrawal. Mrs. Crippen gave notice of withdrawal on 15th December. The money could not be payable to anyone until 15th December, 1910."

That ended the first day of the trial, and, as we left, Holmes gave me a smile. "Dew and our doctor friends will give their evidence tomorrow. Much more interesting. I hope your pencil and notebook will be ready!"

They indeed were as, on the morning of Wednesday October 19th, Chief Inspector Dew took the oath as a witness.

Chapter Eleven

Dew's story you have already read in much detail, so I will spare you unnecessary repetition. But I was interested to hear how Crippen had actually been in the notorious little coal cellar, with Dew, during the chief inspector's first visit to Crippen's house on July 8th.

Tobin asked Dew about it, and Dew replied:- "I said that I should like to go into the cellar, and he came with me."

"No difficulty whatever about it?"

"No."

"Did he show you the smallest trace of worry or anxiety as to going into the cellar with you?"

"He was perfectly cool .... I should think that we would stay in the cellar for about a couple of minutes. It is a very dark cellar. It would be approximately in the middle of the floor that I afterwards found the remains. I do not think there was any coal lying about the floor at the part where I found the remains; I think the coal was at the side of the cellar."

"The part where the remains were subsequently found was, as far as you remember, not covered by coal at all?"

"No, except dust, and perhaps a small portion of coal, but not much."

Crippen apparently remained cool when Dew told him he would now have to find Mrs. Crippen.

"Did he then in any way indicate alarm or fright, or anything of that kind?"

"No, he did not."

Dew related how he visited the cellar again, by himself, on Monday July 11th.

"I looked around and tested the bricks with the heel of my boot. That is all I did, except to look at the floor as far as I could with a candle. I would spend two or three minutes in the cellar that day. I pushed the bricks with my heel to see if they were loose, but I did not find anything to arouse my suspicions. On an ordinary examination, there was nothing to indicate to my eye or to my foot that the cellar floor had been disturbed for years; there was nothing to indicate that there was anything wrong.

"I went back again on the Tuesday and looked all around, examined the rubbish and moved it, and probably tapped it with my foot, but there was nothing to notice."

Dew went on to testify as follows:-

"On Tuesday, 12th July, I made a further examination of the house, and also on the 13th, when, amongst other things, I again searched the coal cellar.

"The coal cellar had a brick floor. There was a very small quantity of coal there, and also a little rubbish, cuttings from small branches of trees, an old chandelier, and such things as that. I went down with Mitchell on to my knees, and probed about with a small poker which I had got out of the kitchen. I found that the poker went in somewhat easily between the crevices of the bricks, and I managed to get one or two up, and then several others came up pretty easily.

"I then produced a spade from the garden and dug the clay that was immediately underneath the bricks. After digging down to about a depth of four spadefuls I came across what appeared to be human remains.

"After digging further, I sent for Dr. Marshall, the divisional surgeon of police in that district, and Sir Melville Macnaghten, the chief of the Criminal Investigation Department. Dr. Marshall came between five and six o'clock, and he saw a portion that I had unearthed. After I had procured assistance, we dug further, and Dr. Marshall came back later on. We left the remains where they were that night, without moving them; we covered them up, locked up the house, and left it in charge of two police officers.

"On the next day, the 14th, Dr. Marshall again attended, along with Mr. Pepper. Under their instructions the remains were removed from the cellar and put into a coffin and removed to the mortuary. In addition to the remains which we put into the coffin there were some articles which we put into a tray, one of these articles being a Hinde's curler. From that time, the 14th July, the remains were in charge of the doctors, so far as I know.

"I made some measurements of the cellar, at the request of Mr. Pepper. The distance from the surface of the brick floor to the upper portion of the remains was 8 inches; the depth of the brick was 3 inches, so that there was 5 inches of earth or clay. The bricks had been laid on the flat. Some of the remains were lower than others; the distance from the upper surface of the brick to these would be 12 inches. All the remains were found within a depth of 12 inches, including the brick within 9 inches of earth."

Under questioning a few minutes later, Dew told Muir:- "In the garden I found a raised heap of earth covered with garden litter and empty flower pots. I caused that to be dug, and I found on the top there was a small quantity of loam or garden mould, and underneath six inches to eight inches of clay, and below that again all loam."

Holmes and I exchanged wry glances. I winced and raised my eyebrows to signal frustration. Holmes responded with a wry smile and a Gallic shrug. We both knew that any contribution that my friend had made to either discovery was *sub rosa* and neither could nor would be mentioned.

Mr. Muir:- "You saw the amount of clay that had been dug from the hole in the cellar?"

The Lord Chief Justice:- "Is not that going a little too far? It is quite sufficient that somebody did find clay there."

The Lord Chief Justice, again:- "I suppose you probed with the poker between the bricks?"

"That is so."

"Was there any mortar between the bricks then or not?"

"It could not be described as mortar; it had been very closely packed down, and was covered with coal dust and that sort of thing. I saw no mortar, and I do not think that any had been used. The clay would keep the bricks very firm."

The chief inspector also mentioned the discovery of the lone pair of pyjama trousers that, as we now knew, were matched the jacket found with the remains.

Dew:- "When I was searching the house on the 14th I found … a box underneath the bed in the first-floor front bedroom. In that box I found two suits of pyjamas and one odd pair of pyjama trousers … I did not find any jacket to correspond with those trousers, although I looked for it."

He did not at this point explicitly mention, nor was he asked about, the jacket found in the grave.

Tobin pursued further details on the discovery of the remains.

Tobin:- "They were rammed in?"

Dew:- "Yes, rammed in, but looser there than in other parts of the cellar where there were no remains. I would describe the remains as close-packed with clay. The cellar was three yards long by two yards three inches wide; the length of the remains was four feet one inch, and the greatest width twenty inches. It was a fairly regular oblong area. The remains were mixed altogether, packed close together in a mass extending over that area. There was lime mixed up with the remains. Of course, as we dug we may have taken some of the lime off the clay."

"Take a bit of flesh there and another bit of flesh below it, might there have been lime between a sprinkling of lime, then some remains, then another sprinkling of lime, and then more remains?"

"No, there was one mass. There would be nothing actually in between; it would all be either at the bottom or at the side. So far as I could judge, the lime was all round the remains, over them, under them, and at the side of them, but not mixed up with them in the sense of layers. There were different bits of skin of different sizes found amongst the remains."

"Mixed up and folded over in parts, jumbled up all together?"

"All together; this huge mass of flesh was all together."

"Were any parts of those bits of skin folded over?"

"I cannot say. It was impossible for me to make such a close examination as that. I found the first lot of remains about five o'clock, and then I sent for Dr. Marshall. They remained there till he came, but I had not taken up much then."

"Then when Dr. Marshall came the remains were taken out?"

"Oh, no, not touched at all. I sent for two police officers with spades and other implements, and we then dug completely round this mass of flesh and uncovered it. We covered that up about twelve o'clock midnight, and locked the cellar door; we left two police officers in charge and left the house. We did not touch the remains at all as far as we could help. We laid some boards over the hole that we had made. Mr. Pepper and Dr. Marshall came about eleven o'clock next day, and they stayed till the remains were removed by an undertaker. They made some examination of them, and then about two o'clock the remains were placed in a shell and removed to the mortuary, and passed out of my care entirely."

Augustus Pepper was the medical witness who first introduced the scar on a piece of the human flesh found buried in the little cellar.

"On the 15th July I found a piece of ... skin, seven inches by six inches, which came from the lower part, the front portion of the abdomen. There was a mark upon that piece which attracted my attention, and I afterwards examined it with particularity. I spent several hours examining it."

Muir:- "In your opinion, as the result of that examination, what was that mark?"

Pepper:- "It was the mark of a scar, a little over four inches in length ... It was quite an old scar."

He went on to discuss the removal of the innards and organs from the torso before it was buried.

Muir:- "Having examined the manner in which the viscera have been extracted from that body, are you able to say whether it was done by a skilled person, or not?"

Pepper:- "Yes, it must have been."

"You mean the extraction from the body?"

"The removal of the viscera from the body. It has been done by a person skilled in removing viscera … There is not a cut or tear in any part except where it was necessary for the removal. It was removed all in one piece. All the organs I have described were connected together, and the diaphragm or the septum between the chest and the abdomen had been cut round. In my opinion that would certainly require skill."

At one point, as the gruesome medical specimens were passed among the jurymen for inspection, one of them became ill and distressed. The trial was adjourned for two hours so that he could receive some attention, and recover.

With the court back in session, Tobin challenged in detail the proposition that the mark on the piece of skin was a scar. Then the Lord Chief Justice weighed in with a question to Mr. Pepper:-

"Now, I want to ask you whether or not you can say that, in your opinion, you have no doubt that this is a scar?"

Pepper:- "I have no doubt … On 9th September I was present at St. Mary's Hospital when a piece of the skin bearing the mark which I say is an old scar was removed for microscopical examination, and I was present when that piece was microscopically examined on 13th September by Dr. Spilsbury. I also examined it myself; the examination I made quite corroborated my previous opinion … I had not the slightest doubt, without examining it with the microscope, that it was the scar of an old wound, and that was confirmed by the microscopical examination."

There also came this vital piece of expert evidence from Pepper:- "I formed the opinion that those remains had been buried from four to eight months. In forming that opinion I took into consideration the place where they were buried, the surrounding materials, the lime and the earth, and the depth at which they were buried. In my opinion they were buried very shortly after death."

Muir:- "In your opinion, is it possible that those remains could have been buried there before 21st September, 1905?"

"Oh, no, absolutely impossible."

The following day, the third of the trial, Dr. Spilsbury agreed with Mr. Pepper.

"As the result of my microscopical examination, I say that that mark is undoubtedly an old operation scar."

Tobin:- "Before you formed your opinion, when you examined it with your eye, you had heard, had you not, that Belle Elmore had had an operation in the lower part of the abdomen?"

"Yes, I believe I had read that in the press ... The fact that I had read in the papers that there had been an operation upon Belle Elmore had no effect at all upon the opinion I have expressed. I have no doubt that this is a scar."

Spilsbury agreed, too, that the viscera had been removed by somebody with 'considerable anatomical knowledge' and 'who has done a considerable amount of evisceration'.

I wondered if the Crown would introduce evidence that Crippen had such experience, but this did not come about.

Dr. Marshall followed, and also testified that the mark on the piece of skin was a scar. "I was with Mr. Pepper on 8th August when he first saw the scar. On that day I formed the opinion that that piece of flesh which had the mark upon it came from the lower part of the abdominal wall. I formed the opinion that it was a scar mark, and that is still my opinion."

Then the hushed courtroom heard Dr. Willcox, the senior scientific analyst to the Home Office, describe as to his vital discovery of the fatal dose of hyoscine hydrobromide.

"I took weighed portions of the stomach, intestines, kidney, and liver, and treated them by the usual process for extraction of alkaloids, with the result that I found an alkaloid present in all these extracts, then applied further tests to see what kind of alkaloid was present. I tested for all the common alkaloids: morphia, strychnine, cocaine, and so on, and I found that a mydriatic alkaloid was present; that is, an alkaloid the solution of which, if put into the eye of an animal, causes the pupil to enlarge and dilate. Having found a mydriatic alkaloid, I applied a further test, and found that it was a mydriatic vegetable alkaloid, of which there are three: atropine, hyoscyanin, and hyoscine. I applied further tests, and found that the alkaloid that I had got in the extracts corresponded to hyoscine. I have no doubt it was hyoscine ....

"In the whole of the organs submitted to me, the amount of hydrobromide of hyoscine was two-fifths of a grain, which would certainly correspond to more than half a grain in the whole body."

Muir:- "What is a fatal dose?"

Willcox:- "From a quarter of a grain to half a grain. Hydrobromide of hyoscine is a drug which is a powerful narcotic poison."

He went on:- "This is not a drug that is commonly used ... As far as I know, it is not used as a homœopathic remedy. I have looked through the English and the American pharmacopœias, and the drug is not used."

Willcox described at length the complicated and time-consuming tests that led him to conclude the fatal drug was hyoscine hydrobromide, and was strongly challenged by the defence on the method and the outcomes of his testing. Dr. Willcox, however, stuck firmly to his work and the finding.

Then Dr. Arthur Luff, Willcox's predecessor at the Home Office, and author of the book *Forensic Medicine and Toxicology*, was called by Muir as a witness.

"I have followed up Dr. Willcox's tests for hyoscine as given in evidence, and I agree that they are absolutely the right test. I have repeated all the tests recently with specimens of the pure drug, and I quite agree with Dr. Willcox that the poison that was present was undoubtedly hyoscine, judging by those tests."

For the defence, Tobin was no more able to shake Dr. Luff than he had been able to rattle Dr. Willcox.

Then the trial turned to Crippen's purchase of hydrobromide of hyoscine in January.

Charles Hetherington, a chemist at Lewis and Burrows, testified that Crippen had placed an order for five grains of the drug in crystal form, rather than in the tabloid form usually purchased by doctors. "I asked him what it was for and, as far as I remember, he stated it was for homœopathic purposes." Hetherington did not have such a quantity of hyoscine available, so ordered it from the wholesaler, the British Drug House.

Harold Kirby, an assistant at Lewis and Burrows, told the court and jury that he handed over the drug to Crippen on January 19th. As a doctor, Crippen rarely signed the poisons register but did upon this occasion, stating therein that the drug was for homœopathic use. It was his first purchase of this particular drug from Lewis and Burrows, although he was a regular customer there.

Throughout all this accumulating and unfavourable testimony, Crippen sat quietly in the dock, showing no emotion.

Adelene Harrison was called as a final Crown witness, and testified (without her habitual extraneous comments) about Mrs. Crippen's hair, her bleaching of it, and the dead woman's under-garments.

Tobin then opened the case for the defence by announcing that Crippen would testify in his own defence, and that medical witnesses for the defence would give their own expert judgment on the supposed scar. Then an expert in poisons would tell the jury that the drug found in the body was in fact a substance produced by the natural putrefaction of the remains.

Offering an important challenge, Tobin went on to propose that the prosecutors had not proved, beyond all reasonable doubt, that the remains were those of a woman, let alone those of Belle Elmore.

Tobin spoke simply and eloquently. "There was an illicit intimacy between Mrs. Crippen and Bruce Miller, and an illicit intimacy between Crippen and Le Neve – the latter might be another reason for Mrs. Crippen's departure. Where was she now? Why did she go? She went because she had long disliked Crippen, and her dislike had turned to hate. "

Therefore, the lawyer argued, Mrs. Crippen left of her own choice, and she told Crippen to cover up the scandal as best he could. That led to his 'campaign of lies'.

Crippen then co-operated with the police, and allowed them to search his house. But then he realised that his lies must have 'raised a mountain of prejudice and formed clouds of suspicion'.

Shaking his head patiently at the jury, Tobin added that Crippen resolved in his folly to fly. "What more natural than that he should take with him his mistress? The rest followed as a matter of course – the disguise, the shaving of his moustache, the dressing of Le Neve in boy's clothes. He went away from the inquiries of the officer as innocent men had fled before."

(Holmes jotted something in his note-book, silently tore out the page, and passed it to me:- 'Of course, guilty men *never* flee.')

Tobin cast further doubt on the scar, on the identity of the remains, on the date on which they had been buried in the cellar; and as for the apparently skilful dissection of the remains, Crippen was 'a man who had never done that work as part of his practice during the whole of his professional work'.

The defence counsel then addressed Crippen's purchase of hyoscine.

"He need not have signed the poisons book at all but openly he left the record of his purchase and his name at a shop where he was known. He bought it to reduce to a liquid, and to use it in the tiny tabloids he prepared for patients."

In conclusion, Tobin asked the jury to decide that the Crown had not demonstrated, beyond all reasonable doubt, that the remains were those of a woman at all, and still less had identified the remains as part of the body of Belle Elmore.

Now Crippen himself took the oath, and calmly spoke of deteriorating relations with his wife after his return to London following a six-month absence while working in America.

"She was always finding fault with me, and every night she took some opportunity of quarrelling with me, so that we went to bed in rather a temper with each other. A little later on, after I found that this continued, and she apparently did not wish to be familiar with me, I asked her what the matter was. She told me then that she had met Bruce Miller, and that he had been taking her out while I was away, and that she had got very fond of him, and that she did not care for me any more."

On the night of January 31st, he said, came a final argument – about whether Crippen should have accompanied Mr. Martinetti, their dinner guest, to the upstairs toilet.

"Mr. Martinetti wanted to go upstairs, and, as I thought he knew the house perfectly well, having been there many times during eighteen months, I thought it was quite all right that he should go up himself. When he came down he seemed to have caught a chill, and after they went away I was blamed for not going up with him. They left somewhere between one and two o'clock, I think; I know I had a lot of trouble to find a carriage for them.

"Immediately after they had left, my wife got into a very great rage with me, and blamed me for not having gone upstairs with Mr. Martinetti. She said a great many things. I do not recollect them all; she abused me, and said some pretty strong words to me; she said she had had about enough of this that if I could not be a gentleman she would not stand it any longer, and she was going to leave me.

"She also said something that she had not said before, that after she had gone it would be necessary to cover up any scandal that there might be by her leaving me, and I might do it the very best way I could."

Huntley Jenkins, a barrister on Mr. Tobin's team, asked Crippen about the hyoscine.

"I have for years been familiar with the drug hyoscine. I first heard of it when I came over to England in 1885; I learned the use of it in the Royal Bethlem Hospital for the Insane. It is used a very great deal in America, especially in insane asylums. It is also used in ophthalmic clinics. I have used it as a nerve remedy in a homœopathic preparation, that is, reduced to extremely minute doses. I remember purchasing some hyoscine on 19th January."

Crippen went on to describe how he made his homœopathic medicines with hyoscine.

"The dose would be in the form of small sugared discs. A dose would consist of two discs, and the actual dose would be approximately 1/3600ths of a grain, extremely minute. That is what I did with this hyoscine that I purchased. I think I dispensed about two-thirds of the hyoscine that I purchased on 19th January. I might mentioned that, besides using it for nerve cases, I also found it useful for spasmodic coughs and spasmodic asthma."

(Another note from Holmes:- 'No evidence that he dispensed *any*. No record of prescriptions or homœopathic preparation. Even if he did, the remaining third was quite enough to poison Elmore. We did not find any left-over hyoscine at all, none, anywhere at his home or his offices.')

Now came up the question of the 'suicide notes' that Dew found on Crippen on the *Montrose*.

One, written in pencil on a piece of card, read:- 'I cannot stand the horrors I go through every night any longer and as I see nothing bright ahead and money has come to an end I have made up my mind to jump overboard tonight. I know I have spoilt your life but I I *(sic)* hope someday you can learn to forgive me. With last words of love. Your H.'

The second, shorter in length, said: 'Shall we wait until tonight about 10 or 11 o'clock. If not what time?'

Dew had told me and Holmes that, taken together, the notes suggested that Crippen had planned to kill himself, or somehow to disappear and leave behind a misleading note to suggest he had committed suicide. Dew was sure that both cards were in Crippen's hand-writing.

Now, in court, Crippen gave this explanation: The notes were, he said, part of an escape plan concocted with a friendly quartermaster of the *Montrose*, a plot, he said, that was known to Le Neve.

"He told me that the captain knew who I was and also who Miss Le Neve was, and that I was to be arrested by the police at Quebec. He also told me that I must leave a note behind me saying that I had jumped overboard, and that in the middle of the night he would make a splash in the water and tell the captain that I had gone. As a matter of fact, I wrote one card that same day, and that night he took me downstairs, but somebody came along and prevented us from going down. They saw us, so I kept that card, and he said he would put me down the next day. I then wrote the short card next morning, just a short time before Inspector Dew came on board.

"The long card was to be put on my pillow in the berth in the cabin. I had arranged with Miss Le Neve, as the quartermaster said that there was no charge against her that they did not want her at all, I had arranged with her that when I got ashore safely I gave her an address in the States where she was to write to me and let me know when everything was all right and she could join me."

Crippen said he had not given this explanation to Dew because one of the Canadian police officers told him that arrest procedures in Canada and England were different, and that, in Canada, he should say nothing to the police. Crippen quoted this unidentified officer as telling him: 'Now don't you say a word on anything; cut your tongue out; have nothing to say'."

(A third note from Holmes:- 'Not true at all in Canada. All quartermasters deny any scheme. Bet Tobin does not call any of them.' He was right; too; the defence did not do so.)

The accused then explained what he had meant when he said to Chief Inspector Dew, 'It is only fair to say that she knows nothing about it. I never told her anything'.

Crippen testified:- "I had never told Miss Le Neve anything about my talking to my wife before she went away about this scandal; I had told her that my wife had gone away, and I told her afterwards that she was dead. These were the only two things that I told Miss Le Neve. Consequently she never knew anything about all these letters and lies that I had disseminated ....

"I do not think my wife knew of my relations with Miss Le Neve, because she always treated Miss Le Neve with the greatest courtesy when she came into my office. There was no obstacle ever put in my way if I wanted to go and see Miss Le Neve. My time was my own; I went as I liked, and I often stayed away from business whole days at a time. I told Miss Le Neve that if ever my wife went away and got a divorce I should marry her certainly."

"Was she perfectly satisfied with the position she occupied?"

"She seemed to be very happy."

Crippen confirmed in court that his wife had a scar from surgery to remove her ovaries. He also confirmed that she bleached her hair and that he 'sometimes helped her'.

The courtroom was hushed as Mr. Jenkins asked:- "Did you ever, at any time, administer any hyoscine to your wife?"

"Never."

"Those remains that were found at your house in Hilldrop Crescent – have you any idea whose they were?

"I had no idea. I knew nothing about them till I came back to England."

The court adjourned for the day, and Holmes and I returned to Baker Street for dinner. We reviewed the proceedings of the day, and Holmes said he thought that it had gone well enough for the Crown. "Dew's 'little beggar' spoke well, though, and between Tobin and Jenkins he gave some explanations that a jury could understand. We can but wait to see how Muir takes him apart tomorrow."

This 'taking apart' began the fourth day of the trial, on Friday October 21st, if much less dramatically than I had hoped for.

Muir:- "On the early morning of 1st February you were left alone in your house with your wife?"

Crippen:- "Yes."

"She was alive?"

"She was."

"And well?"

"She was."

"Do you know of any person in the world who has seen her alive since?"

"I do not."

"Do you know of any person in the world who has ever had a letter from her since?"

"I do not."

"Do you know of any person in the world who can prove any fact showing that she ever left that house alive?"

"Absolutely not; I have told Mr. Dew all the facts."

(Hasty note from Holmes. 'When is Muir going to take Crippen's wicket?')

Muir moved on to ask Crippen about Tuesday, February 1st.

"When did you come home?"

"I cannot say to the exact hour that night, but I generally came home at 7:30; that is my general home hour."

"What time did you come home on that night when you say you did not find your wife there?"

"The nearest, I should say, is it would be my usual time, about 7:30."

"Do you not recollect on that momentous night what time it was when you came home?"

"I would not like to say, It was somewhere near 7:30, it might have been 7:25; it might have been 7:35; but it was close on 7:30."

The judge suggested that Crippen had answered the question, but that Muir could press it further if he wished.

"Did you tell Inspector Dew that you got home between five and six?"

"I do not remember telling him that hour."

Muir now read from the statement that Crippen made to Dew and Mitchell, and signed, on July 8th, 'I came to business the next morning, and when I went home between 5 and 6 p.m. I found she had gone.'

"Is that right?"

"If I said that to him, that was probably right. I cannot trace it back."

(Note from Holmes:- 'Not a wicket, but a good enough ball. Juries find even small contradictions weighty.')

Dew had testified that he had told Crippen that he (Dew) would have to find Cora Crippen, and that Crippen had said that he would do everything he could. As we know, Crippen had suggested an advertisement in American papers, but, having prepared such an advertisement, he had not actually submitted the notice.

Now Muir asked if Crippen had made inquiries of tradesmen or neighbours or local cabmen about seeing Mrs. Crippen and any luggage leave the house.

"I have made no inquiries."

(Note from Holmes: 'The jury will not like that.')

Where did you think your wife had gone?"

"I supposed, as she had always been talking about Bruce Miller to me, that she had gone there. That was the only thing I could make."

"That is to America?"

"To America."

"Have you made inquiries?"

"No."

"As to what steamers were going to America on or about that date?"

"No, I have not."

"At no time?"

"At no time."

"Not since your arrest?"

"Not at all."

"What? Not at any time? Not to find out whether there was some steamer sailing for America on which there was a woman answering the description of your wife?"

"I have not."

"Nobody has made those inquiries?"

"No ..."

"You have made no inquiries at all?"

"I have made no inquiries at all."

(Note from Holmes: 'The jury does not like this. Look at them. Arms folded and severe looks.')

Later in the morning, Muir led Crippen, lie by lie, through what even Tobin had called 'a campaign of lies'. Crippen testified that the untruths had all been to save himself from scandal, in which friends might believe that he had treated his wife so badly that she had left him.

"She told me I must do my best to cover up the scandal and I made those statements for that reason."

Muir pointed out that, according to Crippen's story, he had kept his wife well, and had given her money and jewels and clothes, even though they had not slept together for four years; then she had run away with another man.

"Why should you seek to cover up a scandal for such a wife as that?"

"I do not think I can explain it any further than I have."

Muir asked Crippen what led him to believe that his wife, absent but alive, would not write to her friends.

"I did not believe she would write to anybody, the way she was going on."

"Would she not visit her sisters or step-father in America?"

"I did not think she would ... If she went off with some other man, I did not think she would have the face to go there."

(Note from Holmes: 'Very facile.')

Muir asked if the remains could have been buried in the cellar during the period of five years in which the Crippens lived in the Hilldrop Crescent house.

"Not that I know of, of course."

"So far as you know, that is impossible?"

"I would not say it was impossible, because there were times when we were away; during my absence in the daytime my wife was often away."

At that, the judge broke in. "Do you really ask the jury to understand that your answer is that, without your knowledge or your wife's, at some time during the five years, those remains could have been put there?"

"I say that it does not seem possible. I mean, it does not seem probable, but there is a possibility."

(Note from Holmes:- 'And Father Christmas is real.')

Now Tobin, for the defence, called upon two medical witnesses, who soon presented some remarkably confused evidence on the matter of Belle Elmore's scar. I was sure this had a negative impact on the jurymen. So agreed yet another scrawled note from Holmes.

Dr. Gilbert Turnbull, director of the Pathological Institute at the London Hospital, testified that he had examined the piece of flesh and its so-called scar three times, and he had performed a microscopic examination. "It enables me to say that it cannot possibly be a scar."

He went on to add:- "If that mark ... is not in fact a scar, it was caused by folding of the skin by pressure."

He meant, of course, folding of the piece of skin when the remains were dumped into the grave in the cellar, and were then compressed by having clay and lime loaded onto them, and then by the restoration of the brick floor.

This was not what Mr. Pepper, and Doctors Spilsbury and Willcox had found.

In further testimony, while sticking to his opinion that there was a fold but no scar, Dr. Turnbull opined that the piece of flesh came from the lower abdomen. This agreed with the professional findings of the Crown's doctors.

But, under questioning by Muir, Dr. Turnbull disclosed that when he first examined the sample, "I formed a different opinion as to the part of the body it had come from." Not a 'definite' opinion, he added, but one that he had put in writing for the defence. However, he said, he had not expected to be called as a witness for the defence,

Questioned by Muir, and by the judge, Dr. Turnbull gave what struck me (and no doubt the jury) as a confusing account in which he said he first had doubts that the skin came from the abdomen.

Muir pursued this. "What part does it come from if not the abdomen?"

"From the upper part of the thigh."

But now, he said, after further examination of the flesh, "my opinion now is that it is from the lower part of the abdominal wall."

Dr. Turnbull also spoke of having given the specimen a twenty-minute examination. That stood out for me, and perhaps for the jury, when compared with Pepper's testimony that he 'spent several hours examining it.'

Next for the defence came Dr. Reginald Wall, whose medical career included pathology. He spoke of three lengthy examinations of the flesh, and echoed Dr. Turnbull:- "In my opinion it is not a scar ... I found appearances which I could explain much more easily on the supposition that the skin had been folded in that region."

Dr. Wall went on to admit (in a manner as confusing as that of Dr. Turnbull) that he and Dr. Turnbull had, over time, changed their initial finding that the flesh had not come from the abdominal wall.

"I am quite willing to admit that we have modified that opinion since ... My opinion now is, that it may have come from the abdominal wall, but there is not sufficient evidence to say definitely where it comes from. I think it probably does."

But, he added, "The two parts of the body from which it might be derived, as we thought when we first saw the piece of skin, were the lower part of the abdomen and the upper part of the thigh on the inner side. We reported that in our opinion it probably did not come from the abdominal wall; that is the opinion we have modified."

The Lord Chief Justice asked Wall, "Have you any doubt that it did come from the abdominal wall?"

"I have a doubt in so far as I am not absolutely certain."

"Have you any doubt about it?"

"Yes, I have."

"Where do you think it came from?"

"That is the trouble. If I could suggest where it came from, it might be useful? That is why I said I thought it probably came from the abdominal wall."

(Note from Holmes, as Dr. Wall stepped down:- 'Score all that as five to nil for the prosecution.')

We were told later by the Crown lawyers that Doctors Turnbull and Wall had delivered their initial opinions to

Arthur Newton, Crippen's unscrupulous solicitor, on the understanding that they would not be called as witnesses. Newton then undertook some legal machination to compel them to come to court and testify.

Tobin now called a third doctor for the defence, Dr. Alexander Blyth, author of the text *Poisons: Their Effects and Detection*.

Dr. Blyth proposed that the alkaloid substance found by Dr. Willcox could have been produced by natural putrefaction rather than by poison. "I think there is strong evidence that there is in putrefying tissues a substance very much resembling the mydriatic alkaloids produced."

Pressed hard by Mr. Muir, Dr. Blyth went on to contradict something he had written in his own book, and cited new foreign research as a reason. But he then dug himself deeper into a hole by admitting he had seen only extracts from these foreign studies.

(Note from Holmes:- 'Poor witness. No damage to Willcox and Luff.')

Muir now played the 'finesse' prepared by him and Travers Humphreys – and got away with it. Muir got permission from the judge to re-call Crippen, and to present evidence as to the date on which Crippen purchased the pyjama suit of which the trousers appeared to match the jacket found with the buried flesh in the cellar.

Tobin objected, although it seemed to me that he did so none too strongly. "If notice of it had been given to us we, the defendant's advisers, might have made inquiry into it."

The judge ruled against Tobin. "It is the practice of our law always to give the prisoner every notice that is possible, but in every case in which a point arises as to whether the evidence is material, it is for the judge to say whether or no it is admissible. It does not depend on notice being given."

Tobin repeated that the evidence about the purchase of the pyjamas should not be admitted at this stage, as the Crown could and should have dealt with it earlier.

The judge replied.

"Do not think I am blaming you, but it is Dr. Crippen's own evidence that makes this so material."

Chapter Twelve

Crippen was thus formally re-called as a witness. Muir asked him whether he had purchased the pyjamas in question before or after he moved into Hilldrop Crescent in 1905. (Earlier testimony had established that this move was in September, 1905.)

"I think it was shortly after, because it was only at that time that I began to wear pyjamas."

(Note from Holmes:- 'Got him! Wait until Muir calls our fellow from Jones Brothers.')

The 'fellow from Jones Brothers', William Chilvers, was indeed now called upon. He testified that he recognised the material of the jacket and trousers, and that it had been sold by the company no earlier than November or December 1908.

"We keep sale duplicates. I have here the sale duplicate for 5th January, 1909 ... There are two other items paid for at the time, to the same address: 39, Hilldrop Crescent."

Chilvers went on to confirm that the remains of the jacket found with the body, and shown to the court in a jar, matched the material of the pyjama trousers that were also shown to the court, and that the jacket bore a label from Jones Brothers.

"I have seen the tab on the part which is in the jar; it bears the words 'Jones Brothers, Holloway, Limited.' Jones Brothers have been a limited company since 1906."

I needed no note from my friend to know that these pyjamas, then, did not exist before the Crippens moved into

Hilldrop Crescent, and could not have been purchased by Crippen or his wife 'shortly after' their move.

I also recognised that while Crippen had not agreed that the trousers and jacket were of the same material, Chilvers, as a qualified witness, did confirm that they matched.

Game to Mr. Muir!

Tobin did not challenge Chilvers. "I do not call any other evidence."

And now, for the first time, I heard a judge deliver his 'charge to the jury' in a capital case.

The chief justice began with instructing the jury as to two points.

"The first question is, were the remains found at 39, Hilldrop Crescent the remains of Cora Crippen. If they were not, there is an end of this case. If you find that they were the remains of Cora Crippen, then you have got to ask yourselves, was her death occasioned by the willful act of the defendant Crippen? If not, again the defendant is entitled to be acquitted."

As a third point, the judge noted that Crippen had argued, in his own defence, that his wife had left him. "That is the defence put forward by Dr. Crippen, which you must carefully consider. If made out, you need not trouble any more about who the remains were."

So far, so fair, I decided. But then, I thought, the judge went on to load the dice against Crippen.

"If he is guilty, as you may think, he is, of course, an extraordinary man. He has committed a ghastly crime; he has covered up that ghastly crime, or endeavoured to, in a ghastly way, and he has behaved with the most brutal and callous indifference after the crime has been committed. If he is an innocent man, it is almost impossible, as you may probably think, to fathom his mind or his character, again absolutely indifferent to the charge made against him of murder; having, according to him, I will not say a ready means, but at any rate the means of doing his utmost to establish his innocence, no step taken of any sort or kind by him."

I could but nod in silent agreement with Holmes when he displayed to me another hastily pencilled note:- 'He is inviting them to find Crippen guilty.'

The judge went on to say that this was a court of law, not of morals. If Cora Crippen was an immoral woman at some time, or Crippen was immoral with Le Neve, "you must not visit him or find against him the charge that is to be proved because he is an immoral man or because he is a liar."

The Lord Chief Justice continued.

"What you are entitled to do is to take into consideration those circumstances where they have a direct bearing upon the question of fact which you are considering."

I thought this would be confusing to the jury, and looked askance at Holmes. He merely shrugged.

Later in his charge, the chief justice made the point that Crippen had made no effort to find his wife after her disappearance.

"Of course, one most extraordinary thing will probably strike you – that if Crippen honestly believed that the woman had gone to Bruce Miller at Chicago ... you would have thought that there was one channel at least whereby inquiries might be made of a most important character; and probably the thought has occurred to you, if Dr. Crippen believed that his wife had gone, either for a moral or immoral purpose, to visit Bruce Miller, among her own friends, how is it that no inquiry was made by Dr. Crippen of Bruce Miller?"

Holmes waved gently again his note proposing that the judge was inviting the jury to convict Crippen. I nodded agreement.

My friend repeated this gesture after the judge told the jury that "You must ask yourselves the question, if it is true that the woman left on 1st February, why did she leave the bulk of her jewellery behind her; why did she leave, as far as one can tell, the bulk of her fine clothes behind her – not only the furs which might keep her warm – for they are expensive furs – but furs which were pretty valuable."

The judge went on to address Crippen's pawning of jewellery in two lots, for a total of one hundred and ninety-five pounds. If Crippen had wanted and used the money for his business, as he testified, he could have given corroborative evidence about it. But, as the judge pointed out, "It rests entirely upon the statement made by Dr. Crippen and nobody else."

The judge drove another nail into the scaffold as he reviewed the lies that Crippen told to his wife's friends about her death. "If you come to the conclusion that the game was so enormously dangerous that Dr. Crippen could not have possibly carried it out if he thought his wife might appear again, you will ask yourselves, can you believe the story that his wife left him on 1st February?"

And he hammered in one further nail. "The newspapers in two continents have been full of the case ... If Belle Elmore is alive, is it possible to think that this has not come to her knowledge? Does that man in the dock mean to suggest that so bad is this woman who was his wife for eighteen years ... that she is so mean and so abominably wicked as to allow this man to stand his trial in the dock without making any communication or anything of the kind? That is what you have got to consider in this part of the case."

The judge reviewed the question of identity of the remains in the cellar. "In order to satisfy you that it is not Cora Crippen, the defence must have satisfied you that there is no scar there. Coupled with the pyjama and the camisole and the combinations and the vests, you have to ask yourselves, have you any doubt that that is the body of Cora Crippen?"

(Note from Holmes:- 'He would hang Crippen himself, methinks.')

The judge addressed the poisonous hyoscine. "Someone gave Belle Elmore hyoscine, and she became unconscious, comatose, and died, and there was the dead woman in the house. Where did that hyoscine come from? It may be a coincidence, gentlemen. It is entirely for you. Are you satisfied with the account the defendant has given of what he had to do with the hyoscine bought on 19th January?"

If there was hyoscine left over from Crippen's preparation of medications, where was it? "You must ask yourselves, are

142

you satisfied with that account? He has given his account; it is for you to say whether you believe it; but, in any event, if you are satisfied that hyoscine was in the body, where did it come from?"

Then the chief justice noted that Crippen had promised to take out an advertisement to find his wife. "He never sent it. If he believed that his wife could be found, why should not he have sent it? His answer to me yesterday was 'I thought if I got away they would not trouble about me any more'. That is his idea, I suppose, of English justice."

Finally, the Lord Chief Justice closed with this:-

"I end as I began. If you are of the opinion that his story of his wife's going away on 1st February is true, verdict of not guilty. If you are of the opinion that the Crown have not satisfied you that these were Cora Crippen's remains, poisoned by hyoscine, buried and mutilated, verdict of not guilty.

"But you ought not to hesitate from returning a verdict, if you are satisfied upon the evidence, by any fear, or suggestion, or doubt, as to what might occur in the future. There has been ample opportunity for getting hold of Cora Crippen if she is really alive. You cannot proceed with the case upon the theory that she is alive, unless you believe the defendant's story.

"You will, of course, as I have said, look to the fact that the Crown have got to prove their case. You will give the benefit of any doubt to the prisoner Crippen; but, if the evidence points to the fact that he, and he alone, is responsible for the death of his wife, Cora Crippen, you will not hesitate to do your duty."

As those last words echoed in the courtroom, the jury retired at 2:15 o'clock.

A loud buzz of conversation arose in the crowded courtroom, although the clerk of the court and usher frantically demanded silence. Holmes lowered his voice to a whisper.

"The scar, the hair, the underclothes, the pyjama jacket, all strongly suggest that the corpse was indeed that of Mrs.

Crippen. The remains were clearly buried while the Crippens lived in the house, and not before.

"Crippen buys a large and lethal amount of hyoscine. He says he dispensed some of it, but he offers no accounting for the quantity involved. We found no record at his offices or home of his having actually prescribed or processed any, and we found no remaining hyoscine at his offices or at the house; not a trace. I was a little surprised that Muir did not pursue or press these points hard, but at least the judge did.

"As for the medical evidence, I think we can fairly give that my score of five to nil for the prosecution. The doctors for the defence did no favours at all for Crippen and Tobin.

"Crippen's failure to look for his departed wife, his pawning of the jewellery, the cashing of cheques, the question of whether he had the skills to dissect the body, his amazing string of lies and deceit, and even his extraordinary flight, are things I myself place little weight on.

"The jury probably will be impressed by them, though, and after that summing up and charge, I have little doubt that the verdict is guilty. Dr. Crippen is for the gallows."

I put a hushed question to Holmes. "What about this argument proposed by Tobin that Belle Elmore disappeared on February 1st, some time after 1:30 o'clock in the morning. Crippen then went to work as usual that morning, and Ethel Le Neve was at Hilldrop Crescent the next day, the 2nd. How could Crippen have killed and butchered his wife and disposed of all the remains during that short period; he simply had not the time."

Holmes shrugged. "We have only Crippen's word – only *his* word – that he went to work on the first. His office staff think that he did come to work on the first, and on subsequent days. However, the staff at one of his other establishments believe he did not appear there for the first three days in February. We also have no evidence at all, other than his word, that Le Neve was at Hilldrop Crescent on the second. Indeed, she has told us that she began to spend more and more of her time there 'some days after' the 1st. Not much of a case for the defence."

When my friend pulled out and examined his watch for what must have been the tenth time, I asked him, "How long do you think they will be out?"

"Not long. Perhaps an hour; perhaps two."

To Holmes's nodded satisfaction, and to my surprise, the jury returned to the courtroom after only 27 minutes, at 2:52 o'clock. They began to file solemnly into their positions.

"He's done, then," declared Holmes.

Chapter Thirteen

After a slight delay, Crippen was returned to the dock from the cells below. There was then, suddenly, complete silence and stillness in the court. Crippen stood to attention, perhaps shaking a little. I could just see that his slightly bulging eyes were anxiously fixed on the foreman of the jury.

The clerk of the court spoke first.

"Gentlemen, have you agreed upon your verdict?"

The foreman replied.

"We have."

"Do you find the prisoner guilty or not guilty of willful murder."

The foreman paused solemnly and firmly intoned, "We find the prisoner guilty of willful murder."

A collective gasp went up around the courtroom. Crippen winced, and closed his prominent eyes, his head now downcast.

"And that is the verdict of you all?"

"Yes."

"Prisoner at the bar, you stand convicted of the crime of willful murder. Have you anything to say why the court should not give you the judgment of death, according to law?"

Crippen, although slumping slightly, looked up and responded strongly, "I am innocent."

"Do you wish to say anything?"

"I still protest my innocence."

In the ensuing hush, Lord Chief Justice Alverstone delivered the sentence.

"Hawley Harvey Crippen, you have been convicted, upon evidence which could leave no doubt on the minds of any reasonable man, that you poisoned your wife, that you concealed your crime, you mutilated her body, and disposed piece-meal of her remains; you possessed yourself of her property, and used it for your own purposes. It was further established that as soon as suspicion was aroused, you fled from justice and took every measure to conceal your flight.

"On the ghastly and wicked nature of your crime I will not dwell. I only tell you that you must entertain no expectation or hope that you will escape the consequences of your crime, and I implore you to make your peace with Almighty God."

Then I saw, for the first time, a judge don the traditional and ominous 'black cap'. It was not a cap at all, but a simple square of some heavy black fabric, with one corner hanging down slightly over the centre of Alverstone's forehead.

He delivered clearly the words that we have all read in the newspapers. They echoed darkly in the still-hushed Old Bailey.

"I have now to pass upon you the sentence of the Court, which is that you be taken from hence to a lawful prison, and from thence to a place of execution, and that you be there hanged by the neck until you are dead, and that your body be buried in the precincts of the prison where you shall last have been confined after your conviction. And may the Lord have mercy on your soul."

The attending court chaplain called out 'Amen', and there was again awed silence. The judge thanked the twelve jurymen and sent them on their way. Crippen was taken downstairs to the cells again. The lawyers noisily packed up. their papers. As the courtroom emptied, Dew approached us, and shook Holmes's hand with enthusiasm.

"Holmes, I and Mitchell and the Crown must thank you. I do not hesitate to say that without your help and guidance we might have got absolutely nowhere on this case. Indeed, were it not your astute observation about the clay in Crippen's garden, we might never have found the body, and Crippen would have got away with it."

Now I must tell you that, back on October 25th, Le Neve had gone on trial at the Old Bailey, accused of being an accessory after the fact in the murder of Mrs. Crippen. Again Muir led the prosecution team, but spoke only briefly in his closing speech, and without drama.

Miss Le Neve's barrister, F. E. Smith, argued that 'there is not a vestige of proof' that she knew anything of the fate of Crippen's wife.

The jury agreed, speedily declaring her not guilty. She was immediately freed, and began a sad series of eleven visits to Crippen in Pentonville Prison.

On November 5th, three judges of the Court of Criminal Appeal delivered their decision on Crippen's appeal. Holmes reviewed it for me over dinner.

"Tobin presented four main challenges. First, that the juryman who briefly became ill when he saw the medical specimens during the trial, had not been supervised by a court official when separated from the other eleven jurors. The appeal judges held that since the man had not discussed the trial with anyone, or there was no evidence of that, the incident did not affect the trial.

"The second ground for appeal was Muir's finesse in recalling Crippen to testify about the pyjamas – and thus to introduce evidence about the date of their purchase and the material. Tobin argued that this was improper, and that the defence should have been notified in advance. The appeal court ruled that the evidence was admissible, and that the Lord Chief Justice had the discretion to admit it.

"Tobin went on to a third point, that the Crown had not proved the body was that of a woman, and certainly had not proved it was Cora Crippen. The appeal judges held that there *was* evidence that the remains were those of Mrs. Crippen. Further, the appeal judges said they were not surprised that the jury would prefer the testimony of the Crown's doctors over that of the defence's doctors.

"Tobin's fourth contention was that Alverstone's summing up of the case was in places ambiguous and unclear and, in effect, put the onus on Crippen to prove that the body was not that of his wife, rather than on the Crown to prove that it was. The three appeal judges held that the summing up put the case for Crippen adequately, fully and fairly, and that no injustice had been done.

"All in all, then, the appeal court held that there was ample evidence to support the verdict. Appeal dismissed."

I broke in. "Which means that ..."

"That Crippen will hang on or about November 23rd, unless the Home Secretary accepts a plea for a reprieve."

On the same day as the appeal, Chief Inspector Dew submitted his retirement papers, with his last day at Scotland Yard set for December 5th.

If the authorities had been plagued before the arrests with false sightings of Crippen and Le Neve, they now were plagued with fraudulent letters from people claiming to be Mrs. Crippen and alive. The penmanship of least one of these, I know, was compared with the writing of Mrs. Crippen and was quickly declared to be a fake, as were the others. The authorities also received (and, of course, instantly rejected) the startling offer of a retired soldier to be hanged in place of Crippen.

Defence solicitor Newton sent a petition for a reprieve, signed by some fifteen thousand people, to the Home Secretary, Mr. Winston Spencer Churchill. Mr. Churchill rejected it.

And on November 22nd, Le Neve made her last visit to Prisoner Number 9146 in Pentonville prison. Crippen's last words to her, we learnt, were 'Goodbye, and God bless you'.

We also learnt, by way of Chief Warder Joseph Bostock, an old friend of Holmes, that Crippen had made out a will leaving everything to Miss Le Neve.

And at nine o'clock in the morning of Wednesday, November 23rd, Crippen was hanged.

Holmes and I needed no creative newspaper reports of the execution, for we had the story straight from John Ellis, the hangman, three days later. We met at the Brecknock Arms, a public house on the Camden Road that Crippen had favoured, near his Hilldrop Crescent home and not far from Pentonville Prison. This was Ellis's idea as he was 'just curious.'

"Crippen was right nervous in his cell, of course, as they all are as the last morning approaches. He was crying a lot during the night, and we think he may have planned to kill himself during the night watch. He had deliberately broken his glasses and concealed a sharp piece in his trousers. Warder Fellows caught him at it, though, and made him surrender it. Mr. Fellows and the other warder kept a right close watch indeed on Crippen during the rest of the night.

"But Crippen looked strong enough, and he was even smiling in the morning as William (you know my assistant, William Willis, Mr. Holmes) tied Crippen's hands behind his back and I pulled Crippen's shirt wide open. I gave him a pat on the shoulder and told him, 'You'll be all right, sir', the way old Marwood used to do in his day. And Crippen smiled. He seemed to be quite a pleasant little fellow, you know.

"I went ahead of him to the topping shed. He was still smiling when the chaplain and the warders and William brought him in. No hesitation, no collapse, no struggle; just a normal walk, quite fast.

"With his last words, he thanked the governor for his courtesy and kindness at the prison, and for allowing him visits and letters from that Le Neve girl.

"I could see that Crippen was still smiling as I pulled a new hood over his head and William quickly strapped Crippen's ankles together. I set the noose on him nice and proper, new rope, all the stretch taken out, got my nod from the governor, and I pulled the lever. The bolts get pulled, the trap goes thud, and Crippen goes down. Just one minute from the time William and I went into the condemned cell.

"A drop of seven feet, nine inches, neck properly broken, and as clean a job as I have ever done.

"Our second topping in two days, it was, and then a third at Reading."

Ellis was so casual about all this that I winced. He did not seem to mind at all. Holmes slipped him two guineas. "Thank you for delaying your journey home, Mr. Ellis. We had much wanted to hear how it all went."

Crippen's shady solicitor, Arthur Newton, quickly became involved in a lurid scandal as to whether Crippen had made a confession. Newton apparently claimed there *was* such a confession, and offered it to *The Evening Times* for a thousand pounds, then settled for five hundred. The newspaper published what purported to be the confession. It was written in the third person, which the newspaper explained by saying Crippen had confessed to 'a friend' who had supplied an account of it to the newspaper. It was a sparse and unconvincing document in which, for what it is worth, Crippen supposedly confessed to having fed his wife 'indigestion pills' that he had made up with hyoscine, and to having carved her up with a surgical knife.

It soon became clear, however, that the confession was an outright fake from beginning to end. Prison officials denied that there had been any confession at all, and word spread in legal circles that this so-called confession, and another soon published in *John Bull*, were fictions concocted for cash by the crafty Newton. Newton simply admitted nothing, and refused to clarify the issue, one way or the other. The Law Society later suspended him, specifically over the letter of purported confession in the *John Bull*.

All the London newspapers were quickly full of, if not a confession, the love-letters that Crippen wrote to Le Neve from the condemned cell at Pentonville. These, we understood, had been sold to the newspapers by Miss Le Neve. In one, Crippen appeared clearly to confirm the earlier speculation that, at some point, Le Neve had been pregnant and miscarried:-

'If only I could have left you well provided for, I would have wished our little one had lived that you might have had what would have been part of both of us.'

The letters were full of warm (and overly warm) expressions of love to his 'Dear wifie, greatest love of my heart and soul', and the very last letter closed with this:-

'These are my last words. I belong no more to the world. In the silence of my cell I pray that God may pity all weak hearts, all the poor children of life, and His poor servant.'

(The newspapers were also full of the collapse of the Charing Cross Bank in which Crippen and his wife had money on deposit. The bank had defrauded depositors of well over two millions of pounds, and at least two impoverished clients committed suicide as a result.)

Dew kindly read the notes and the drafts that I prepared for a potential series of magazine articles on the case. He was polite enough, and helpful, but told me firmly that I had not given enough credit to Holmes for building the case against Crippen.

Holmes, in turn, insisted that I had not given enough credit to Dew and Mitchell. "Muir was very hard on Dew and in my view criticised him unfairly." It seemed that Muir might have, in effect, joined the school of thought that held that Dew should have arrested Crippen before he fled. Holmes shook his head, angrily. "And what would he have arrested him for? For lying to his wife's friends? Obviously, that is no crime and, equally obviously, Dew at that point knew of no crime for which he could have arrested and held Crippen."

As Holmes packed his belongings to return to his bees, and I packed my own bags to go home to Southsea, Dew gave his last words to us on the case.

"You know, if Crippen had not aroused suspicion with his flood of lies to the music-hall people, and all that nonsense with a black armband and so on, he might have got away with it. I would never have been called in.

"And if he had not immediately run away, he might still have got away with it.

"If he had stuck firmly to a story that his unfaithful wife must have run off to some American lover, if Crippen had told us and the music-hall people that he never wanted to see or hear of Belle Elmore again, well, it would all have been believable. If he had extended the lease on the house, and simply carried on life with Le Neve, he could have pulled it off. I had said I would try to find his wife, and so I would. But for how long? And how hard? How long would it be before I dismissed the case as simply that of a woman who had left her husband and did not want to be found?

"And if the variety people had come to us weeks or months down the road and said that they could not find her anywhere in America, and that nobody anywhere had seen her again, there or here, we would probably have replied that, as an adult, she was entitled to disappear if she chose to. We cannot hunt endlessly for every person who disappears. We have files upon files of people who have been reported as missing. Many we never find."

Holmes broke in. "Another mistake, to go with all that: Look at the way he dissected the body, removed the head and the limbs and the sex organs, filleted all the bones from the torso, and somehow got rid of the lot, all successfully. And then he buried the last remains in his coal cellar. Why do that? Why not dispose of the flesh as he had disposed of the other parts of the body? Come to that, why not dispose of the whole body at one go? Another huge mistake."

Dew shook his head, stretched his arms wide in puzzlement, and continued Holmes's theme.

"And why not dispose of *all* her clothes and jewellery? Why leave so much lying around where we or others could see it, and wonder why she had left so much behind? I know he burnt some of her clothing, and also gave some away, but could not have simply have given the whole lot away, in one move, to some women's charity?

"Do you know one more thing that did him in? Guess what: his failure to order in a ton or two of coal to cover up the grave and the brick floor. If that cellar had been full of blessed coal I might never have given it a second thought. Even the clay in the garden might not have lit the fuse; there were other areas and piles of clay that I saw, throughout the garden.

"But when you, Holmes, wondered if something had replaced the clay, my thoughts went straight to the cellar. Thank heaven that they did, and that we did manage to track down and arrest Crippen.

"In my retirement, I shall long hear the Lord Chief Justice's words 'Hanged by the neck until you are dead.'

"And rightly so."

Author's Afterword

A tribute to Walter Dew and Arthur Mitchell

Apologies to Walter Dew and Arthur Mitchell for my giving to Sherlock Holmes so much credit for building the case against Crippen.

Police tradecraft at the time was basic, and thin. Forensic sciences were in their infancy, DNA science and testing were unknown. There was a traditional, heavy reliance on simple observation, and unscientific witnesses.

Dew and Mitchell and their team did what they could with what they had, and Crippen was caught and hanged as a result.

Still, there is one little question that remains to be cleared up for me: Which policeman first wielded the poker to begin digging up the remains in the cellar?

According to Dew's sworn testimony: "I went down with Mitchell on to my knees, and probed about with a small poker which I had got out of the kitchen. I found that the poker went in somewhat easily between the crevices of the bricks, and I managed to get one or two up, and then several others came up pretty easily."

He repeated this story in his autobiography, *I Caught Crippen* (see the list below of books consulted.) "I was armed with a poker, and with this worked away, too tired to say a word. Presently a little thrill of excitement went through me.

The sharp point of the poker had found its way between two of the bricks, and one of them showed signs of lifting ... The brick came out. Then another and another."

But author David James Smith in his 2005 book *Supper with the Crippens* (see also the book list below) reports that he found in the case papers in the National Archives a statement by Mitchell himself. It included this:

"We then went into the coal cellar, and on probing the brick floor, which was covered in coal dust, I dug the poker between two of the bricks in the centre of the floor. I loosened and removed them, and Chief Inspector Drew then dug the floor up, and uncovered some pieces of human remains as described."

So, who really used the poker? It's an issue I have 'written around' in the book.

It is true that Crown prosecutor Richard Muir accused Dew at one point of 'sleepy sickness' in pursuing the case. But what Muir meant has never been entirely clear.

Some suggest Muir meant that Dew should have arrested Crippen at the beginning, and should never have let him escape to the continent and on to Canada. But I find no record of Muir saying or hinting at this.

Dew wrote in his autobiography: "I came in for criticism. Certain people with no knowledge of police procedure and less of the law blamed me for allowing Crippen to go. I ought to have arrested him, they said. Ridiculous! There was up to this time no shred of evidence against Crippen on which he could have been arrested or even detained. Futile to talk of arresting a man until you know there has been a crime. No person can be charged with murder unless the body, or some portion of the body, or some very strong evidence that murder has been committed, is available."

Muir, of course, was fully familiar with both the law and police procedures, so is unlikely to have pointed to the lack of speedy and premature arrest as a deficiency.

Others have said Muir found that Dew had made insufficient effort (or no effort at all) to pursue evidence from Jones Brothers about the pyjama jacket found in the Hilldrop

Crescent grave. If so, again, Muir did not put this on record. I have written around this issue as well, of course.

Note: Some readers may be confused by Dr. Watson calling Augustus Pepper, a fully qualified doctor, 'Mr.' rather than 'Dr.' This is because Pepper was a Fellow of the Royal College of Surgeons and a consulting surgeon. The use of 'Mr.' for such doctors is an old British tradition, dating from historical times when the early surgeons became qualified through apprenticeship and diploma, rather than through a university degree.

The DNA Mystery

In 2007, forensic biologist David Foran of Michigan State University announced that DNA tests on what he said was a sample of the Belle Elmore remains determined that the tissue sample was (i) not genetically related to Belle Elmore; and (ii) was actually from a male.

Foran started with one of Bernard Spilsbury's microscope slides, clearly marked 'Crippen' and 'Scar in skin'. From it, Foran and team isolated mitochondrial DNA, which remains unchanged throughout the generations down the female line. Meanwhile, a genealogist had come up with people she said were grandnieces of Cora Crippen, who would have the same mitochondrial DNA as her, by way of a half-sister of Cora.

Foran's team used new techniques to examine the nuclear DNA, and discovered a male Y chromosome. "Not only was the body not from Cora Crippen's family, it wasn't even a woman."

You'll find much more on this story, written by Foran himself, in *The Scientist* magazine at https://bit.ly/2nclJqq.

All this led Crippen's closest living relative in 2007 (retiree Patrick Crippen of Dayton, Ohio) to say the British government should grant Crippen a posthumous pardon.

But Foran's findings have since been questioned: For one thing, were the 'grandnieces' *really* relatives of Cora Crippen? (The genealogist who found them insists they were.) Was the male Y chromosome actually from Spilsbury or one of his assistants, who prepared the slide? Was the slide what Foran thinks it was? While labelled 'Crippen' and 'Scar in skin', was it mislabelled?

And if the remains *were* those of a male, how come 'he' had been poisoned with hyoscine, buried in Crippen's cellar during Crippen's tenancy, along with hair like Mrs. Crippen's, a hair curler like Mrs. Crippen's, women's underwear like Mrs. Crippen's, and with a pyjama jacket of a type owned by Crippen?

Regardless, there has certainly been neither sign nor hint of any pardon from Westminster.

Aftermath

Walter Dew, after retiring on his police pension (and winning hundreds of pounds in damages or settlements from nine newspapers that he sued for libel) indeed became a private investigator. He retired to Worthing, and died on December 16th, 1947.

Ethel Le Neve quickly ducked out of sight after Crippen's execution. She spent some time in Canada, working as a typist in Toronto, then quietly returned to England. In 1915, while working at a London furnishing business, she married clerk Stanley Smith. They lived in Croydon, and had a son and a daughter. Ethel died in Dulwich Hospital on August 9th, 1967.

No. 39, Hilldrop Crescent, was hit by German bombs on September 8th, 1940, and was later demolished as beyond repair. The site now is occupied by a block of flats, Margaret Bondfield House.

The £250 reward went to Captain Kendall of the *Montrose*, who did not cash it, but framed it as a souvenir. My apologies to the memory of Captain Kendall for my attribution to Sherlock Holmes of Kendall's idea that Dew be disguised as a pilot to come aboard the *Montrose* off Father Point.

About Spelling and Grammar

As in my previous 'Dr. Watson' book (*The Adventure of the Bloody Tower, The Irregular Special Press for Baker Street Studios Ltd., Sawston, Cambridge, 2013)* I have tried to stick to the spellings and grammar that the good and educated doctor would have used in 1910. Thus I have used 'ise' (recognise, realise, advertise, theorise) rather than 'ize', as 'ise' was much more likely in Britain in 1910. However, I do note that *The Strand Magazine* of the era used both spellings, inconsistently.

Note: I have used 'Marsinger' as the spelling of the surname of Mrs. Crippen's American stepfather, as that was used in a transcription of Crippen's formal statement to police, and in the *New York Times*. Various other sources use Mersinger, Marsangar (as in the official 'Wanted' notice from the Metropolitan Police) and even Haraanger (in a badly mistyped public copy of a court transcript.)

Books Consulted

Douglas G. Brown and Tom Tullet, *Bernard Spilsbury*, George H. Harrap & Co., 1951.

Nicholas Connell, *Walter Dew: The Man Who Caught Crippen*, Sutton Publishing, Stroud, Gloucestershire, 2005.

Max Constantine-Quinn, *Doctor Crippen*, Duckworth, London, 1935.

Tom Cullen, *The Mild Murderer: The True Story of the Dr. Crippen Case*, Houghton Mifflin Company, Boston, 1977.

Walter Dew, *I Caught Crippen*, Blackie & Son, London and Glasgow, 1938.

Colin Evans, *The Father of Forensics*, Berkley Books, New York, 2006.
Michael Gilbert, *Dr. Crippen*, Odhams Press Ltd., London, 1953.

Jonathan Goodman, *ed.*, *The Crippen File*, Allison & Busby, London and New York, 1985.

James H. Hodge, *ed.*, *Famous Trials 10*, Penguin Books, Harmondsworth, 1964.

Gordon Honeycombe, *The Murders of the Black Museum 1870-1970*, Hutchinson Ltd., London, 1982.

H. Paul Jeffers, *Bloody Business: an Anecdotal History of Scotland Yard*, Barnes & Noble, New York, 1999.

Erik Larson, *Thunderstruck*, Crown Publishers, Random House, New York, 2006.

Ethel Le Neve, *Ethel Le Neve: Her Life Story; with the true account of their flight and her friendship with Dr. Crippen; also startling particulars of her life at Hilldrop Crescent / told by herself.* Publishing Office, London (probably 1911).

Jane Robins, *The Magnificent Spilsbury and the Case of the Brides in the Bath*, John Murray (Publishers), London 2010.

David James Smith, *Supper with the Crippens*, Orion Books, London, 2005.

Filson Young, *ed.*, *The Trial of Hawley Harvey Crippen*, William Hodge and Company, London, Edinburgh and Glasgow, 1920.

Katherine D. Watson, *Dr. Crippen*, The National Archives, Kew, 2007.

Novels Consulted

Val Andrews, *Sherlock Holmes and the Hilldrop Crescent Mystery*, Breese Books, Baker Street Studios Ltd., Sawston, Cambridge, 2011.

Richard Gordon, *The Private Life of Doctor Crippen*, William Heineman Ltd. London, 1981.

CPSIA information can be obtained
at www.ICGtesting.com
Printed in the USA
LVHW032227031019
633101LV00013B/686